A Boy Of Bruges: A Story Of Belgian Child Life

Emile Cammaerts

A BOY OF BRUGES

A Story of Belgian Child Life

BY

EMILE AND TITA CAMMAERTS

With Sketches
BY
ALBERT DELSTANCHE

NEW YORK
E. P. DUTTON & COMPANY
681 FIFTH AVENUE

U V

ANNETTE'S SONG

[*Page* 118]

TABLE OF CONTENTS

LIST OF ILLUSTRATIONS

A BOY OF BRUGES

A LETTER TO THE ONE WHO READS THIS BOOK

DEAR SCHOOLMATE:

If you think that I am putting a story of Belgian children into our storybooks for American boys and girls because the United States helped to save Belgium from starvation during the Great War, you are quite mistaken. I choose the nations for our Schoolmate Series, not because we send gifts to them, but because they bring gifts to us. And Belgium's gift is priceless. For Belgium is feeding our souls, and we shall live in the strength of that spiritual food so long as memory lasts. Because Belgium has laid down her life rather than break her word, no other nation will ever again be able lightly to break faith with its fellows. It is harder to tell lies since Belgium made her stand for honesty. And Honor shines a brighter word since Belgium burnished it with her blood.

Out of our millions of bushels of wheat we have given a few bags of flour, which we do not need for ourselves, to feed Belgium; but she has given her very self, her life, that the world might be fed. It is this gift of her quickening spirit that we Americans treasure; it is by this gift that Belgium is helping us to make honorable citizens out of the boys and girls who were at school in the United States when the Great War broke out in Europe.

Before the war, we did not dream that little Belgium would one day bear an important part in the making of American citizens. We knew there were Belgians in our great Melting Pot, intelligent and industrious people; but compared with the Italians and Russian Jews who were coming over from Europe, and the Germans and Irish who had already come, the Belgians were few in number. How many Belgian children were there in your school before the Great War? Not many, I am sure. Perhaps none at all, unless you lived in a large mill town like Lawrence, or Lowell, Massachusetts, where wool and cotton are woven into cloth. The Belgians have been noted cloth-weavers these many hundreds of years, and a few of them, from time to time, have found their way to New England, hoping to earn more money for their children. But it is not always numbers that count most in the making of citizens. Even if after the war no more Belgian immigrants come to us, the influence of their brave self-sacrifice will linger in American hearts; and their story will be told by American fathers to American sons, for many a day.

Belgian history goes back a long way, to the days of Julius Caesar, who found the Belgæ sturdy fighters. And as we come down the centuries we find them again and again doing their bit for civilization. In the eleventh century, when the First Crusade set out for the Holy Land on that romantic adventure, the freeing of the Holy Sepulchre from the infidels, two of the leaders, Godfrey of Bouillon and Count Robert of Flanders were Belgians, and Godfrey was made the first King of Jerusalem. And in 1204, at the time of the Fifth Crusade, another Belgian, Baldwin IX, Count of Hainault, was crowned Emperor of

the East at Constantinople, in the Church of
St. Sophia.

But greater than her military glories are the
glories of her arts and industries of peace,
although she had to do some hard fighting to
gain freedom for her artisans. As early as
960 A. D., there seem to have been cloth
markets in the chief Belgian towns, and wool
was sent over from England to be woven into
the famous Flemish cloth, by the weavers of
Flanders. And it was these Flemish artisans
who rose up in the early fourteenth century
and fought the Battle of the Golden Spurs, to
keep Flemish Belgians from being annexed to
the French monarchy. Armed with pikes,
these workmen of Flanders defeated an army
of double their number, from the chivalry of
France. And it was Jacques van Artevelde,
the son of a great cloth merchant of Ghent,
who brought about the signing of treaties with
France and England, in June, 1338, through
which the Flemings got the right to trade
freely in both those countries. He and his son
Philip dreamed and fought for the independence of Flanders and the freedom of the great

merchant cities, and the great Guilds or companies of merchants and workmen which spread from Flemish Belgium into England and Germany and France.

In modern Belgium, those old trade guilds gave place to trade unions and coöperative groups in which the workmen were banded together in the old struggle for freedom. In their coöperative stores they were able to buy more cheaply and to live better on their low wages, for their wages were the lowest in western Europe, before the war. Yet, according to Mr. R. C. K. Ensor, an Englishman who has written a short history of Belgium, the working class lives better, in some respects, than the same class in England. They know how to get better food for little money, and to. cook it more appetizingly than the English working people do; and they know how to take better care of their clothes; they mend and patch them more skillfully and wear them more tidily. And besides being such hard-working and careful artisans and laborers, they are also good farmers. Before the war had laid waste the Belgian land, the agricultural production per acre was the highest in Europe.

Others besides the workingmen and the warriors have been a part of Belgium's glory. Her women lace-makers have been noted for ages. She has had her painters,—Rubens, Van Dyck, Van Eyck, Teniers,—a noble list. She has her poets. Every child who has seen "The Blue Bird" has heard the name of Maeterlinck. And in the roll call of her kings, the names of Godfrey, King of Jerusalem, and Baldwin, Emperor of the East, are dim beside the splendor that shines from the name of Albert.

The Belgians who come to this country bring with them these gifts of theirs, the sober industry, the practical intelligence, the instinct for coöperation,—for working together toward the welfare of the group,—the thrifty habits, the dignified self-respect, the simple, noble sense of honor. It is for us to cherish them and develop them an hundredfold.

Affectionately yours,

FLORENCE CONVERSE.

The Minnewater

I

BRUGES

THE house in which Pieter was born was one of the quietest in quiet Bruges. It overlooked the Quai du Rosaire and, from the windows of his mother's bedroom, on the first floor, the boy could see some old men leaning over the bridge, the white swans sailing on the canal and the distant tower of the Belfry.[1]

Every note of the carillon could be heard distinctly in Madame Segers's house, although the sound of the bells came faintly veiled when the wind blew from the sea. To the boy, standing silent at the window, it seemed as if

the whole town waited for the chimes, as if
the few people who passed over the bridge and
along the quay, from time to time, had nothing
else, in the whole world, to do, but to listen to
the brazen notes scattered regularly from the
top of the tower, every quarter of an hour.
And each time he heard them, he thought of a
blustery autumn afternoon, when he had seen
the fruit trees in the garden shaken by the
wind, and Marianne running here and there,
gathering the pears in her apron. Were not
all the houses, kneeling around the market-
place, like a crowd of peasant women, and
their red-tiled roofs like so many aprons held
up to catch the falling tones?

The clatter of the sabots or the heavy boots
of the rare passers-by on the uneven cobble
stones, and the occasional barking of a dog
far off broke the silence only to intensify it.
Grass grew in the street, forming neat little
green squares, and the passing of a cart, which
shook the old house, was such an event that
it brought Pieter running even from the bottom
of the garden to his observation-post, where
he lingered, with his ten finger tips and his

nose flattened against the window-pane, long
after the cart was out of sight, wondering if
his uncle the Captain were right after all, and
if there really existed somewhere in the world
large towns whose streets were full of ve-
hicles and whose rivers were full of boats.
But he shrank instinctively from such an idea,
as from some dreadful nightmare, and, in his
own unconscious way, he loved the stillness
which brooded over his native town like a
mysterious but beautiful dream.

It was in this large room, whose three windows took up the whole breadth of the house,
that Pieter Segers had spent his babyhood.
His widowed mother, whom he had never
known but as an invalid resting on a low
couch in a corner of the room, was not able
to take him for walks, and Marianne, their
servant, was too busy cleaning, washing, cook-
ing, managing the whole household, to devote
much time to him. So that, except for an occasional Sunday afternoon walk towards the
Minnewater or one of the old doors of the
town, the outer world of little Pieter was for
years limited by the frame of his favorite

window and by the high walls of the long narrow garden.

When, in later years, the boy shut his eyes and tried to recall his first youthful memories, he met the pensive look of his dog Carlo, whose loss was the first real grief he suffered. Carlo was a small "griffon"' with large beady eyes, which showed a white crescent when he looked up at his master, and long ruffled moustache like an old grenadier-guard. He followed Pieter about the house, sat by his side at dinner, with a napkin tied under his chin, and invariably slept curled up on his eiderdown. From the early morning, when a lick of Carlo's tongue roused him from sleep, till late at night, when he saw the small silhouette perched at the end of his bed, like some familiar spirit, the boy was never apart from the dog, and an intimacy grew up between them which no grown-up could have quite understood.

In spite of his somewhat solemn appearance, Carlo was full of fun and mischief, and brought some sunshine into the otherwise grey life of little Pieter. He had a way of cocking his head on one side and sticking his little rose-

leaf tongue out of the corner of his mouth
which would have tempted the most subdued
and quiet child to set out for some frolic—
not always of a harmless kind. The dog
forced himself like a little Puck into the almost
convent-like life of the family, and the two
women knew only too well who was to blame
when the linen hanging on the line or lying
on the grass—that immaculate linen of which
Marianne was so proud—was found in a
muddy heap at the bottom of the garden, or
when some dish of dainties, which had been
carefully set aside, was prematurely cleaned
with suspicious little lines running across,
made by no grass cloth.

When the two accomplices were confronted
with their crimes, the boy at once betrayed
himself by his flushed face, and stammering
excuses, while the dog assumed the most innocent expression, wagging his stubby tail, prick-
ing his pointed ears, and looking as if he had
never even heard of meadows or larder. But
neither Madame Segers nor Marianne was de-
ceived by such brazen insolence.

This was the origin of the tragedy.

As long as Carlo was quite a puppy, he had
been spared the whip in consideration of his
youth, and for the sake of his master's en-
treaties. But, as he grew, the necessity for
some chastisement made itself felt more and
more, and one day, after the mysterious disappearance of Madame Segers's Sunday bonnet, of which a few feathers were traced to
Carlo's basket, judgment was passed, and
Marianne was obliged to act as executioner.
The boy, who, for once, had been absolutely
innocent, pleaded in vain.

Whether the necessity of showing herself
pitiless stirred her into excessive efforts, or
whether the dog's pride had been abnormally
developed by months of weak indulgence, it
is impossible to say. The fact remains that
Carlo, after bearing his thrashing stoically,
without a grunt or a cry, fled through the half-
open door, as soon as the punishment was over,
and shot like an arrow over the bridge towards the centre of the town. His anxious
master, followed by the repentant Marianne,
at once gave chase, but, in spite of all their

efforts and all their inquiries, the dog could never be found again.

Madame Segers explained that he must have been stolen and Marianne's suspicions were centred around a company of gypsies who were, at the moment, passing through Bruges with a troup of performing dogs, but Pieter would admit no such explanation. For him, Carlo had been hurt in his dignity, just as a child could have been, and would never consent to live under the same roof as his executioner. Nothing that the women could do comforted the boy, and for weeks after, when he passed before the baker's shop at the end of the street, where an announcement was posted concerning the loss of his friend, he had to make the greatest effort to control his tears. He felt utterly wretched and miserable, especially at night when he missed the warmth of Carlo's body against his feet. Sometimes he dreamt that the dog had come back and, when awakened, he burst out crying as he realised the vanity of such hope. He could not get back to his old solitary games, now that for months he had enjoyed his little friend's

company, and he remained sometimes for hours
sitting on a chair his eyes far away, his feet
dangling in the air, brooding over the catas-
trophe which had wrecked his life.

Madame Segers observed with some dismay
these symptoms of depression. The boy was
not strong and had already had several dangerous illnesses. She consulted the old family
doctor who was, at the same time, the best
friend she had in the town. Father Mestdagh, as he was called, shook his wise old
head, took a pinch of snuff which he judi-
ciously absorbed first through the right then
through the left nostril, and replied after a
long pause:

"I will tell you, my dear madame, what is
wrong with little Pieter, and why he grieves
so bitterly for the loss of his dog. That child
needs company."

"But he is nearly always with me."

"Exactly. A sick-room is about the last
place in the world where a boy of eleven ought
to be. You have brought him up wrapped in
cotton-wool. You never give him a chance for
a good romp. Send him to school."

"To school!" Madame Seger's voice trembled and her eyes filled with tears. "He is all I have left in this world. Do you want to take him from me?"

"My dear madame," and the tone of the old doctor softened as he laid his hand on hers. "My dear madame, no one realises better than I do, the grief which this separation might cause you. But it becomes every day more urgent that the boy should have companions of his own age. Think of the future. You will not always be there to look after him."

"You believe that I am selfish in keeping him for myself?"

"Not in the least. I am sure your motives are disinterested, but they are short-sighted. A day will come, sooner or later, when little Pieter must face the world. Not the fairy world which he has built for himself in this room, but the harsh world outside. He will have to fight his way through it, like every other man worthy of his salt. I ask you, will he be equipped for this fight if he remains here?"

"If only his father were there. . . ."

"If his father were there, it would not perhaps matter so much. It is precisely because the boy will not have the support and the guidance of a father that I take it upon myself to advise you in the matter. Besides, I do not want to intrude on your private affairs. It is the boy's health which worries you. It is for the boy's health that I am responsible. I cannot, I will not write another prescription for him. Pieter lacks company. There is nothing else the matter with him. The dog did him good. A playmate would have been still better. He will never be well as long as you keep him here. I know that a doctor's advice is seldom followed, but he has to give it whether it suit the humour of his patient or not——"

"Dear Dr. Mestdagh! . . ."

"I really cannot help it, madame. I am very sorry if I cause you any pain. But I have told you this again and again. Take whatever course you choose, but do not consult me about the boy's health any longer." While he spoke, Father Mestdagh had taken his hat and stick

from the corner of the room and prepared
to go.

"My dear friend," cried Madame Segers,
"you know I always listen to you. . . ."

But the old man would not be detained. He
went out of the room in a flash of temper and
left Madame Segers, who had never seen him
angry before, more worried and more per-
plexed than ever.

On the same night, after Marianne had put
Pieter to bed in the next room, the two women
held a council of war. The boy who had been
awakened by the wind howling through the
chimney followed with keen interest their conversation. He guessed that important matters,
concerning him, were being discussed, and he
listened eagerly holding his breath whilst his
heart was beating in his throat.

"I really do not know what to do," he heard
his mother say. "I never saw old Mestdagh
so much in earnest. But I hate the idea of
sending the child to school, among all these
rough boys who, I am sure, will bully him
and make him perfectly miserable. I admit
that there is something in what he said. . . ."

Marianne was a very quiet woman. She
had a blind adoration for her mistress and
could not bear to see her miserable. At the
same time, she was too sensible not to see that
little Pieter could not much longer remain
isolated from the rest of the world. She had
watched the child more than once playing with
imaginary companions in the garden, calling
them by their names, talking with them aloud,
and she had felt for him deeply. Besides,
Carlo's sudden disappearance still weighed
upon her conscience. The boy heard her
shuffling her feet uneasily, as she always did
when she had something on her mind and
could not find the words to express it. She
finally murmured in a low whisper:

"What about Mathieu, madame?"

"Your little boy?"

"Yes, he is nearly Pieter's age. Only one
year older, though he looks more, having been
brought up in the country. No later than yesterday I received a letter from his grandfather
telling me that he was getting on so well at
school and that it seemed a pity to keep him

in the village where he could never be taught properly. . . ."

"You suggest that he should come over here!"

"Well, madame, it is just as you like. But he would be very kind to little Pieter, I know. He is not a rough child, though a little peasant, rather gentle even. The summer holidays begin next week. Perhaps you would like to try, for a month or so, and see how they get on together."

"Thank you, Marianne, it is very good of you to suggest it. But I should not like to do anything. . . . Should your father agree?"

"Of course, he loves the boy. But if I told him that he should receive a better education in Bruges, he would give way at once."

"Yes, they could play together, and work together. That would be company indeed. . . ."

"And, you see, madame, later on, if they went to the school, and if the boys wanted to bully little Pieter, Mathieu would not let them. He would be like an elder brother to him. Mathieu is pretty strong."

"Write at once, my dear Marianne. Yes,

that would arrange everything. Write at once.
Do not lose an hour."

The boy heard Marianne close the door,
wishing his mother good night, and his heart
stood still: "He would be like an elder brother
for him," he whispered, and he smiled looking
up through the window, while the first stars
gleamed in the dark blue sky.

"Quai aux Herbes"

II

ENTER MATHIEU

THE day of Mathieu's arrival made a land-
mark in Pieter's life.

For a week, Marianne had been busy pre-
paring the house. It had been arranged that
the two boys should sleep in a little room ad-
joining Madame Segers's which had served
before as a store-room. Odd pieces of furni-
ture, baskets full of books, a few birdcages,
old pictures blackened by age and dust, a hundred odds and ends which the conservative
spirit of the housewife retains in the Belgian
home, "because they might be useful some

day," had to be removed and carried into the granary. Pieter stood by pretending to help, taking stock of these unknown riches—the store-room had always been closed for him—and thinking how glorious it would be to roam through the vast granary and to explore the picturesque curiosity shop when Mathieu came.

When Mathieu came. . . . Since the night when he learned about the coming of his new friend, the boy had thought of nothing else. He would not go out or take any pleasure, thinking it mean and selfish to enjoy himself without Mathieu. He saved his weekly pennies in order to spend them with his future friend. With the true instinct of childhood, he loved the boy before having ever set eyes on him, he felt that this affection would be the absorbing enthusiasm of his youth. There was something pathetic in the way he set apart any gift which was sent him at that time. He would not look at a new book with which an old lady, a friend of his mother's, presented him, and he went so far as to resist the temptation of opening a parcel addressed to him by his uncle—which is about the most heroic sacrifice a child can make on the altar of friendship.

"When Mathieu is here." . . . Every time the thought came to him, and that was about every minute of every hour of every day, it seemed to him that a new life was going to begin, or rather that his life—which appeared already very long, as long as *he* could remember—was divided into two stages, the first one before Mathieu's arrival, the second one after his arrival. He felt as if he were going to pass from a small house into some wonderful garden, as if he stood on the threshhold, dazed with the brightness of the sun, the perfume of the flowers and the song of the birds.

He did not speak much of this to his mother or to Marianne. He was naturally shy and reserved and morbidly afraid of being laughed at even by them. But he dreamed of it at night. Mathieu appeared to him in shining garments, like the prince of a fairy tale. He was good, he was beautiful, he was amazingly brave and recklessly bold. He did all that Pieter had longed to do: he rode on horseback,

he jumped over hedges, he waved his sword in
the face of roaring giants and walked calmly
over the dead bodies of huge dragons.

All this would have been enough to cause a
little disillusion to a less imaginative child.
Not so with Pieter.

At last the little room was made ready. The
two narrow beds were rolled on each side,
against the wall, and covered with immaculate
counterpanes; the white and blue curtains were
hung at the window overlooking the garden,
the table was placed in the centre, a few frames
were arranged symmetrically over the mantel-
piece, and the small wooden and copper crucifix, with its twig of blessed box,* nailed at the
head of each bed. The walls were covered
with a flowered paper with garlands of roses
climbing to the ceiling. It was a calm and
cheerful little room and Marianne was very
proud of it. So, of course, was Pieter. In his
joy at seeing it ready, the boy forgot his usual
reserve and tried to pierce the veil of reserve
which enwrapped Mathieu's manifold perfec-
tions.

"Now, how do you think he will like it?"

He was standing in the midst of the room, his face and hands gray with dust, rubbing perplexedly his right foot against his left leg.

"Well, if he does not, he had better not come and tell me," replied Marianne, her head plunged in the cupboard whose shelves she was dusting.

"I am afraid Bruges will bore him," replied Pieter following the trend of his thoughts.

"Why should it?"

"I don't know, everything is so silent here."

"His grandfather's farm is still more lonely."

"Yes, but there are the dogs to play with, and the hens and the cattle to watch, and then . . . there is Annette."

Marianne stopped, gaping, her fists on her hips, and turned on him abruptly:

"What do you know about Annette?"

"You told me yourself some time ago."

Marianne shrugged her shoulders and resumed her work without answering. She never mentioned her small daughter to anybody because she never ceased to worry about her. Annette was a year younger than

Mathieu, a frail imp of a girl, with narrow
bending shoulders, and the doctor had declared
that she could not, on any account, leave the
Ardennes' hills. One day when he had found
Marianne sobbing silently, her face covered
with her apron, Pieter had heard of the child
who was suffering, at the time, from an at-
tack of bronchitis. Since then, that was more
than two years ago, he had never mentioned
her name, knowing full well that it would only
grieve Marianne. The uncanny memory of the
boy amazed the woman; she could not understand how he could remember Annette and
why, if he remembered her, he could have kept
so long silent about her.

But, to-day, Pieter meant evidently to carry
his inquiries even further. He had posted
himself close to the window and was drawing
patterns with his finger on the window-pane:

"Annette could not come, of course?"

"No, she could not."

"Will he be very sorry to be away from her?
Do you think that I shall be able to fill up the
gap?"

"Of course, you will."

"And what about her? How does she take it?"

This time, Marianne could no longer control her temper. In her joy, she had almost forgotten that her little daughter might be made miserable by the new arrangement. It was not only the idea itself which grieved her, but the fact that it had been brought home to her by a stranger:

"Monsieur Pieter, let me tell you! You know too much, you know too much!"

And out she went slamming the door behind her, leaving Pieter still rubbing his right foot against his left leg and drawing with his fingers on the window pane. The drawing illustrated his thoughts. On the top of a hill was the farm, with the chimney smoking, and on the threshold stood a little girl, easy to recognize through her long flowing hair, waving good-bye to some mysterious traveller. When Pieter could not or would not speak, he drew roughly what he meant. It had been, from early childhood, a kind of second language with him.

At last, the great day arrived. It was a

beautiful September day, and, as the evening
glow enveloped the town, Bruges was wrapped
in gold from the top of her belfry to the last
dead leaf floating on the canals.   Madame
Segers, not being well enough to leave her
room, Marianne and Pieter went alone to meet
Mathieu at the station.   It had been arranged
that the boy should travel alone from St.
Hubert and that Captain Dierx, Pieter's
uncle, should meet him in Brussels and put him
in the right train for Bruges.   That Mathieu
should have been allowed to make this long
journey by himself increased still more
Pieter's admiration for the character of his
future companion.   A twelve-year-old boy
must prove very reasonable indeed in Belgium
to be given so much freedom.

"I only hope nothing has happened to him,"
sighed Pieter excitedly trotting beside Marianne along the narrow street leading to the
station.

"Oh! he will be all right, do not worry,"
answered Marianne hurrying on.

Marianne had an awkward habit of quickening her step, when flustered by anything, so

that panting little Pieter could scarcely follow
her. She pretended not to be in the least con-
cerned.

"Mathieu always gets along somehow," she
added after a few minutes, not without a touch
of pride. Still she hastened towards the station whose clock could be seen at the end of
the street.

Railways have, from the beginning, played
a most important part in Belgian life. Some
people, however, can still be found, in the
provinces, who are not yet accustomed to them
and for whom stations, engines and trains are
all part of a new dreadful world with which
no liberties may be taken with impunity.
Madame Segers and Marianne had always
made a rule of propitiating the jealous spirit
of Progress by being at least half an hour too
early when they had to take or to meet a train.
This tradition was inspired both by a vague
belief that the spirit would prove unkind to
them, if they did not pay him this compliment,
and by a healthy distrust of the official time-
table. In spite of numerous experiences, they
could never admit that trains should arrive

at certain stations and leave them at the same
hour every day. What if they took it into their
heads to arrive or to leave earlier? Better,
then, to err on the safe side.

So it was that when they got to the platform
of the Brussels train, Marianne and Pieter
were informed by a smiling official that they
had another forty minutes to wait. They began to pace the platform up and down, but
their waiting did not remain long undisturbed.
First, an express train rattled through the
station, shaking the ground as it passed, and it
took some time to reassure Pieter who believed
that Mathieu was in it and was being carried
away at lightning speed towards Ostend.
Then one or two local trains stopped, releasing
numerous passengers from the neighbouring
countryside, and Marianne scanned their faces,
trying to discover among them the red cheeks
and bright eyes of her boy, while Pieter ran
here and there like a frightened bird, flushed
with anxiety. The same smiling official had
to reassure them and to explain that, though
this was the Brussels platform, every train
stopping here did not come from the capital,

"Besides, look at the clock, it is still too early." But needless to say, this last argument had very little influence on Marianne's almost superstitious belief that trains had an uncanny way of turning up at most unexpected hours. She had still to learn, that, if the engine never takes any liberty in Belgium on this side of the time-table, it frequently does on the other. In fact the Brussels train arrived ten minutes late. As it stopped panting alongside the platform, Marianne and Pieter, taught by experience, posted themselves at the gate through which all passengers had to pass to reach the town, and waited breathlessly for the little traveller to appear.

At one moment, Marianne, stretching her neck, cried: "There, there, I think I see his hat!" But Pieter was no longer looking. He bent his head, his eyes were swimming and he was biting his lips.

"No, Marianne, he won't be here. He is not in the train!"

"How can you tell? You never saw him."

It was true, Pieter had never set eyes even on a photograph of Mathieu, but a sure instinct told him that the heavy-jawed, thick-lipped fellow could not be his friend. If he did not know how he looked exactly, he knew at least how he should look. Not necessarily like the Mathieu of his dreams, but something approaching that delightful vision.

Marianne was too deeply disappointed to pay much attention to the incident. The last straggler had passed through the gate, the station was now again deserted. It became evident that Mathieu had missed his train. The smiling official who had begun to take interest in the strange couple, told them that they had better go back, as the next express-train from Brussels arrived only after midnight. A small boy could not possibly travel at such a late hour. He would surely spend the night in Brussels and come on the next day, in the morning.

In spite of Pieter's protests, they turned their steps homewards. Marianne did not walk fast this time, but had nevertheless to call the boy more than once. He lingered behind, looking over his shoulder, hoping against hope to see Mathieu running after them and hailing him as his friend.

They got home at last and reported to Madame Segers. It was decided, between the two women, that they should wait until the next morning before wiring to the Captain. A wire was only to be used, according to them, in case of life and death. They had a strong prejudice against the Telegraph-Office, as if wiring brought ill-luck.

But Pieter knew better. Thinking it over, he had come to the conclusion that Mathieu would arrive by the midnight train, and he decided to go and meet him at the station. He did not mention his project, knowing that he would be prevented from putting it into execution if he did. He kept his own counsel and, when the whole household was sound asleep, he slipped out of bed, dressed in the dark and descended noiselessly the creaking steps. Then he stopped. In one way, he felt conscience-stricken. Passing her door he had heard his mother stir in her bed. What would she say when she heard of this expedition? The idea of her grief was more bitter to him than that of any punishment. She had a way of looking at him when she was sad, and whispering: "Pieter, oh, little Pieter, I did not expect it of you," which made him very miserable. But, at the same time, he felt sure that his friend was coming, that, meeting nobody, he would wander aimlessly through the town and be exposed to all sorts of accidents, perhaps kidnapped by Gypsies like Carlo, perhaps drowned in the canal. It was his duty to go. He could not do otherwise. Why did the grown-ups never consider a boy's advice, why did they look upon him as of no account?

So he thought, breathless, leaning back against the front door and looking wildly in the deserted street. His heart was thumping in his throat. It was the first time that he had faced the night in this way. It was rather a kind night. A tepid wind blew the faded leaves along the street, a full-moon was rising above the roofs and, on the bridge, at the foot of the statue of the Holy Virgin, a small red lamp was burning. But it was night nevertheless, full of mystery, full of unknown dangers, silent and lonely.

A church clock close by struck twelve. The call was answered almost at the same time by eight or ten clock-towers. Mathieu was perhaps already waiting for him. Pieter took a deep breath, closed his fists and began to run.

It is one thing for a little boy of eleven, to saunter through a town, held by a friendly hand, among the familiar traffic of the streets in full daylight—but to confront the darkness alone, without a guide! Pieter ran through the deserted streets, as if in a nightmare. The shutters were closed, no light filtered through the windows. It was as if the houses had shut their eyes and gone to sleep. Even the street lamps were out at this late hour. Without the help of the moonshine, the boy would have lost his bearings at once. But the deep pools of shadow disturbed him. By this time, he was panting and so hot that he felt the perspiration trickling down his back. As he ran, he saw a faint light at the window of a café. He was on the point of asking the people there to help him. They were talking loudly in a cloud of smoke and, in a corner, an old man was singing. Pieter did not dare to show himself, and ran away faster than ever. He had taken the wrong turning and no longer recognized the street. Then the excitement of this wonderful adventure ceased suddenly. He stopped dead, seized with a great fear. There he was, lost, in the middle of the night, in an unknown quarter of the town, and he would not be able to help Mathieu, who must have left the station by now. He tried to control himself and to think it all out.

He had crossed the market place. It was the shadow of the belfry which had disturbed him so. He must have turned to the right instead of to the left. Now if he turned to the left again, he would surely find his way. He tried to walk steadily and whistle to encourage himself, but he did not finish the tune. This time, he was sure of it, somebody was walking behind him. Or was it his heart beating? No, the steps drew nearer. Not daring to look, he ran. But the stranger ran also. He ran faster and faster. The stranger did the same. To his horror, he felt a hand on his shoulder. Summoning all his courage, he turned on his enemy, ready to strike, like a

They strolled peacefully as if the whole town belonged to them.

fawn at bay. And there, with his bundle on his shoulder, in the full moonlight, laughing heartily, his eyes dancing with mischief, stood Mathieu as Pieter had always imagined him.

The shock was almost too strong. Pieter pinched himself again and again to make quite sure that it was not a dream. He must have looked funny, at the moment, with his blue eyes wide open and his mouth gaping, hatless, breathless, his reddish hair stuck to his brow. He was deadly pale when he stopped. He was flushed now like a peony.

"Mathieu!" he cried, "is it you, Mathieu?"

The elder boy stopped laughing at once. It was his turn to remain dumbfounded.

"Yes," he murmured, "yes, my name is Mathieu, all right. But how do you know? I ran after you to ask my way. I seem to be lost."

"So was I," said Pieter with a sigh of relief. He passed his arm under the arm of his friend, and they walked away together as happy and secure as if they had been in their own garden. They managed somehow to reach the market-place, and the full moon which stood, at that time, exactly on the top of the belfry, looked smilingly at the two little boys who strolled peacefully across the square as if the whole town belonged to them.

*Windmills in
Flanders.*

III

FLEMING AND WALLOON

THE boys enjoyed themselves so much that they did not go straight home. Pieter, who had lost any suspicion of fear since he felt the rough little hand of Mathieu in his own, thought it his duty to show his new friend some of the sights of the town, the belfry and Notre Dame, the Hospital and the "Minnewater." Mathieu followed him patiently, somewhat dazed by his long journey and awed by the dream-city, bathed in the milky moonshine, draped in the shadows of her houses, her pools and canals glittering in the light.

How different was this town, all blue and
silver, with her bells and her swans, her willows and her towers, from his native country
village in the hilly Ardennes, in the midst of
the woods, in the loop of the rushing river!
He had been to Namur several times and once
even to Liége. All was movement over there,
movement and variety. The hills, the winding
rivers, the rustling woods, the peasants hailing
each other from field to field, the workmen
hustling along the street. This town seemed
to be always silent, always peaceful like the
nave of a church, like the castle of the Sleeping
Beauty. And, as they went along, he lowered
his voice to a whisper.

He had long ceased to laugh at the strange
appearance of his companion. Pieter also was
very different from the boys he knew. His
large blue eyes, his pale pinched face, his soft
white clinging hands, were new to him, new
and, in a curious way, pathetic and appealing.
He felt much stronger physically. He wanted
to protect the little stranger, but he followed
him wherever he chose to lead him. He felt
the strength of his new friend's weakness.

Mind you, Mathieu did not say these things to himself in so many words. He was much too young and much too tired to express himself clearly. He walked under the spell of new discoveries and would not have broken this wonderful dream for the world. Mathieu had not much imagination, but one does not need much imagination to be carried away by Bruges, at midnight, in bright moonshine. Let those who doubt it makes the experience.

And so they arrived at home at last, hand in hand, and they rang the bell once, twice, three times, until Marianne's head, in her night cap, appeared at the top window and they heard her run down the stairs.

Why should I describe what followed? We all know what Marianne would do, we all have a dear Marianne somewhere who knows how to kiss and scold at the same time, how to ask questions without waiting for the answer, how to worry about our health when we feel very well indeed, and how to force us to swallow hot soup when we want to go to sleep. Mariannes are the same all the world over, on both sides of the Atlantic.

Pieter was dreading his mother's reproaches but she almost forgot his pranks when she saw the two boys enter her room hand in hand. "Old Father Mestdagh was right after all," she thought. "The boy needed company." Her tremulous voice accompanied them to the door as Marianne was hustling them to bed.

"Go to sleep now, my children, sleep well, my little ones!"

Mathieu needed no encouragement. Scarcely had his head touched the pillow when Pieter heard the regular breathing of the sleeper. In vain did he try to renew their interrupted conversation. A weak groan answered him first, then silence followed. He was forced to postpone all that he had still to say to his friend and, kneeling on his bed, with eyes fixed on the copper crucifix on the wall, he thanked God from the bottom of his heart for having given him his "brother Mathieu." That was his only prayer that night.

Now I do not want the reader to imagine that this friendship between the two boys was all sentimental worship, on the one part, and all chivalrous generosity, on the other. Small

boys are not saints. Pieter had a temper, he
was rather self-willed, self-conscious and
touchy, like most children who have been
isolated for a long time from their kind.
Mathieu was patient with him up to a certain
point. But, when his patience was exhausted,
a dangerous look came into his eyes and he
was inclined to use *striking* arguments. We
must not forget that the two friends had been
brought up very differently, in very different
surroundings. Pieter was a little pampered
"bourgeois"￼ a trifled spoiled by his mother;
Mathieu was a little peasant accustomed to
the rough ways of village urchins. But children have a splendid disregard for class distinction. They know better than to value
somebody by the importance of his income or
of his connections. Unless deliberately trained
to do so, they never judge a man—or a boy—
by his clothes. They judge one another on
their accomplishments. When Mathieu succeeded in shaking the old pear tree at the bottom of the garden, which had till then appeared
to Pieter as immovable as the tower of the
belfry, the latter recognised his companion's

superiority—especially whilst he ate with him the juicy yellow pear which had fallen from the top branch. When, on the other hand, Pieter drew for Mathieu a picture of Marianne, sitting in the armchair beside the kitchen stove, the little peasant was struck dumb by his skill.

The world would certainly be a better world if this simple way of appreciating things and men, according to their real value, to their real abilities, were preserved in grown-up men and women.

No, it was not the difference of class which caused any quarrel between the boys. Pieter never remembered that his friend was the son of his mother's maid. Mathieu never envied this "brother's" beautiful clothes and toys. A boy remains a boy whether his hands are hard or soft. He belongs to the great republic of childhood where distinction and titles are of little or no account if not backed by efficiency.

The only subject on which the friends agreed to differ was the respective qualities of their native provinces. Mathieu was a Walloon and belonged to the Southern part of Belgium

where the people talk either French or a French
patois.⁵   Pieter was a Fleming, as all true
bourgeois should be, and, though he understood French perfectly well, the Flemish language, or if you prefer it, the Dutch language,
was more familiar to him.   Southern Belgium
is hilly and, in some parts very wooded.
Northern Belgium, or Flanders, is a vast plain
covered with meadows and ploughed fields.
The pine and the birch are the trees of the
South, the willow and the poplar those of the
North.   In the Ardennes, the cottages are built
of grey stones and covered with thatch or
slates; in Flanders, they have brick white-
washed walls and red tile roofs.   The costumes
differ from one part of the country to the other,
so does the character of the people.

These differences became a constant subject
of discussion between the two boys.   It began
on the third day of their friendship, as they
were strolling through the fields outside the
picturesque Porte de Gand.   They were standing on a mound at the foot of a windmill and
Pieter, taking his part of guide seriously, was
pointing out to his friend several villages

whose white and red cottages were partly screened by rows of waving poplars. Huge white clouds were sailing along, torn by the sunbeams. The wind was so strong that they had to take their hats off in order to prevent them from sailing away. Towards the north, above the green fields, against the horizon, one could faintly see the golden lines of the sand dunes against the blue sky.

"And beyond that is the sea," exclaimed Pieter, licking his lips. "Do you taste the salt?"

"Yes," said Mathieu, turning round. The plain stretched around them on every side. The mill turned faster above their heads.

"What are you looking for?"

"The hills."

"The hills? There are no hills in Flanders. What should we do with hills? Is it not fine? Wait till you see the sea."

"Hills and woods are fine, too," said Mathieu dreamily.

"Yes. I have seen posters in the station. It looks all so cramped. It must feel as if they were going to tumble on you. I like the sky."

"You have plenty of it at home when you get on the top."

"That means always climbing, always up and down. It must be tiresome."

"Of course if you can't walk. . . ."

"I did not say tiring, I said tiresome. Can you not understand?"

"Your French is not very good you know."

"Neither is yours."

They were both right in a way, most Walloons and Flemings having a strong accent.

"Besides," added Pieter, "it is not my language."

"And what is your language, I should like to know?"

"Flemish."

"Flemish is not a language like French."

"You say that because you don't know a word of it."

"I don't choose to. I don't care to."

"It is not good enough for you, I suppose? Neither is this country. I ought to have known better. I was a fool to bring you here!" And Pieter, flushed to the tips of his ears, walked homewards, not waiting for Mathieu, who followed sulkily. At the Porte de Gand, he noticed the little Fleming who was buying some apples in a shop. He passed the door, pretending not to see. But Pieter ran after him.

"Mathieu! Mathieu!"

"What is it?"

"I've bought you some apples."

"Thanks, I am not hungry."

"Come, let us eat them together. It is not yet time to go home. They look very good. Perhaps they come from the Ardennes. Maman told me that *your* apples are so good, better even than ours. Just taste, you are sure to know."

Mathieu ate the apples sitting in the grass, on the bank of the ditch surrounding the town . . . and they avoided the burning subject for the rest of the day.

At night, when Marianne had left the boys together after blowing out the candle, Mathieu heard Pieter turning in his little bed. He was still conscience-stricken.

"Mathieu, are you asleep?"

"Not quite."

"I wanted to tell you. I have behaved like a beast."

"That's all right, old chap."

"No, it is not all right. How could I speak of your hills? I have never seen them."

"How could I speak of your Flemish. I do not know a word of it?"

"Should you like to understand? I do not mean to speak yourself, just to understand what other people might say?"

"Certainly, if you will teach me. . . ."

"And would you care to walk in the Ardennes with me? I am not strong but I can walk, you know. I should love to climb the hills with you."

"All right, we will. Perhaps, next holidays, You ask your mother."

Another silence.

"Mathieu?"

"Yes?"

"You are no longer cross are you?"

"Nonsense! Don't be an ass."

"Then, shake hands on it."

"I want to go to sleep. If you say another word. . . ."

"You won't shake hands?"

Mathieu's pillow flew across the room, Pieter's followed suit. Amid shrieks of laughter, the fight went on for some time, till they heard Marianne knocking on the floor above their heads. They could not disregard this warning. Mathieu fell asleep on Pieter's pillow and Pieter on Mathieu's, and the moon, peeping through the window, found them, a few minutes later, resting contentedly, smiling in their sleep. Mathieu, no doubt, dreamt of the sea in the North, and Pieter of the woods in the South. Walloon and Fleming were reconciled.

So ended this first quarrel, but it was not the last. Such quarrels stimulate friendship between boys. Each time they made it up they felt more clearly that they could not be *really* angry with each other. They should never have had the pleasure of giving way, if they had always agreed. It is a poor friend who only loves a friend because he agrees with him. A clean fight sometimes brings people nearer.

to each other than a whole life of mutual worship.

Boys understand these things. I only wish grown-ups did.

The Athénée

IV

AT SCHOOL

THE arrival of Mathieu was to be only the first stage of Madame Segers's new scheme of education. Doctor Mestdagh had advised companionship, Uncle Dierx urged school-life.

The captain had called at his sister's house, during a flying visit which he paid to his Bruges relations. He was a true soldier: a man of few words and prompt action.

He arrived by the twelve o'clock train, lunched at half past, cross-examined the children from two to three and left by the four o'clock train after having persuaded his sister that the boys could not be left idle any longer and that, unless they were immediately sent to school, they would become the laziest and most ignorant urchins in the town.

This cross-examination had been a severe trial for them. Mathieu had not been very well taught at his village school, and Pieter's knowledge was limited to the few elementary notions which the good sisters of the neighbouring convent had been able to drill into him. He was lamentably weak in science and geography, of which Captain Dierx seemed to make a special feature. When asked if the Congo flows into the Atlantic or the Indian ocean, Pieter watched his uncle's smiling eyes and concluded that he was setting a trap for him, so he answered: "In the Pacific," which caused the captain to roar with laughter, and to tickle him till he rolled on the carpet convulsed in hysterics.

This incident brought the examination to an end. The boys were dismissed from the room whilst Captain Dierx twirled his black moustache and ejaculated under his breath: "Pacific indeed! Wait a minute, I am going to pacify you!" He had a way of rolling his eyes fiercely which terrified Mathieu.

"Angry?" said Pieter, as they were taking refuge in the garden, "he is not in the least angry, only I am afraid, we are in for it."

"For what?"

"The Athénée."

The "Athénée," in Belgium, means more or less what the Lycée means in France. It is the large State secondary school which can be found in all the principal towns and where boys of all classes are taught, for a very modest fee, from the age of eleven to the age of eighteen. According to their philosophical or political opinions, people send their children either to this State school or to one of the colleges kept by the Jesuit fathers, education being usually of a much lower standard in the private schools and especially in the boarding schools.

The "Athénée" of Bruges is a building of rather forbidding aspect close to the Sainte Anne Gate, on the bank of the main canal. More than once had the boys stopped before its door and wondered at the hidden world beyond. They had heard the bell ring at noon

and at four o'clock and had seen the crowd of
unruly "athéniens" streaming into the street
and hurrying away, as fast as they could, from
the mournful walls.

To Pieter and Mathieu it appeared more
like a prison than anything else. To go to
school meant for them to give up their walks
and their games in the garden, to be shut indoors from eight to twelve in the morning,
and from two to four in the afternoon, without
being allowed either to talk or to run. They
looked upon it as wild birds must look upon
cages, and the delights of Arithmetic and
Latin Grammar were but poor compensations
in the face of such gloomy prospects. The old
porter, with his black skull-cap, his red nose
and his bunch of keys rattling in his hand,
looked exactly like the traditional gaoler, as he
appears in picture books. He was the stern
Cerberus* of this sterner Hades.

They had heard some reports from Pieter's
cousin who had called at Madame Segers's a
few weeks before. And these reports increased their instinctive distrust of the place.
There seemed to be a constant state of war

between the guardians and the prisoners, I
mean, of course, between the teachers and their
pupils. Pieter's cousin had indulged in some
doubtful stories about an unpopular master
who had been obliged to relinquish his post
through the persecutions inflicted upon him by
the boys, persecutions in which the narrator
seemed to have played the principal part.
They had locked up the master's desk, so that
he could not get at his books. They had broken
all the windows in his school-room, so that
he should get a chill. They had sung the
"Marseillaise'" during one of his lessons and
hoisted the revolutionary flag, on the top of
the blackboard. As Mathieu had remarked
that this behaviour was not generous, considering that the master could not raise his hand
to his pupils, the big boy had snubbed him,
declaring that the man deserved his punishment, as he had one day kept the class as late
as six o'clock, and behaved generally like a
most cruel and ruthless tyrant.

Anybody else would have taken these wild
stories with a grain of salt. Not so, our two
inexperienced friends. They listened to them

as we might listen to the report of an explorer who had discovered a new island. It was the first news which they had received from behind the "Athénée's" door, news not likely to be questioned or forgotten.

When Pieter and Mathieu at last crossed the threshold of their new world and were able to judge the school from within, they very soon corrected the wrong impression caused by these legends. They soon noticed that the masters were the last people to be feared in the place. Even those whose temper had been spoilt by many years of monotonous work, without hope of advancement, were easy to please if one only took the trouble. There was, nevertheless, something true in the idea that the school's atmosphere suggested the gaol. Pieter especially suffered from the enforced silence and the long hours of immobility. He had always been free to speak when he liked, to run where he liked. The necessity of sitting at a desk for hours on end weighed heavily upon him. Only one or two hours a week were devoted to physical exercises. The remainder of the time,—with the exception of the regular holidays, Tuesday and Thursday afternoons and, of course, Sunday,—was devoted to lessons: Latin, French, Arithmetic, History, Geography and the rudiments of Natural History. When the sun was out and when Pieter could see, through the high windows, the top of the chestnut trees in the courtyard nodding in the breeze, his spirit left the stuffy schoolroom and wandered abroad, beyond the walls, beyond the town's gates, far away towards the sea.

"Rosa, rosae, rosae . . ."

"Go on, Segers," broke in Monsieur Lambin's voice.

In vain did Mathieu prompt: "Rosam . . . rosam. . . ." Pieter was sailing in a fishing boat with a brown sail, dancing on the waves. "If one went straight along, one could get to England, perhaps even to America?"

"Dreaming again, Segers? Where are you, my boy?"

"In a boat, sir. . . ." This was greeted by an outburst of laughter which rather ruffled Monsieur Lambin's countenance.

"I dare say. You might have been in a

battleship, for all you care!" and his voice became dangerously nasal.

"I am sorry, sir." Monsieur Lambin after meeting Pieter's genuine blue eyes, turned his back on the culprit, shrugged his shoulders, and the lesson went on.

School life would have been very dull without Monsieur Lambin, the principal master of Class VII, into which the two boys had been drafted on the day they entered the "Athénée." He taught them French and Latin and it was with him that they spent most of their time. He was a small, stooping man, with the hooked nose of a bird of prey and the grey vague eyes of a dreamer. He was quite bald, very absentminded, and he wrote poetry in the local paper under the pseudonym of "Spera." He had accumulated an enormous knowledge of classical and French literature and used even to quote Goethe and Shakespeare in the original. Very shy and reserved with his colleagues who patted him on the shoulder patronizingly, he grew sometimes eloquent with his pupils. The children knew his weakness for literature and soon encouraged his wild digressions by insidious questions.

That same summer afternoon during which Pieter had been found out wandering in a boat, was devoted, for instance, to an impromptu lecture on the subject of "The Rose through European Literature." Mathieu had got as far as "rosarum" and was vainly trying to find out which of the many datives with which he was prompted from all sides could be the right one, when Pieter came to the rescue. He lifted his hand impatiently:

"What is it, Segers?"

"I have a book at home called the 'Romaunt of the Rose,' sir, it is very old. I cannot understand a word of it."

The diversion being somewhat abrupt, M. Lambin gazed at the boy suspiciously.

"Why do you say that? It has nothing to do with Latin grammar."

"No, sir, but, as you know everything, I thought you could tell us about it. I have meant to ask you for some time."

A sympathetic murmur from the whole class accompanied this wily explanation.

"It is very hot to-day, sir," whispered a small boy, close to the master's chair. M. Lambin glared at him, then a wistful expression came into his eyes. He also was hot and tired, very tired of the monotonous drill. He paused, one moment, wondering, took his red handkerchief out of his pocket, blew his hooked nose so energetically that his glasses fell on his desk, got up, took a long breath like a diver before jumping into the sea, and walking up and down the room began his lecture. It was an extraordinary lecture for children of that age. He told them of the difference between old and modern French, of the symbolic poem of Guillaume de Loris and Jean de Meung, of Ronsard's love poems, of the mystic rose in Dante's "Paradiso," and of many other things. Nearly half an hour had passed when, after quoting Hugo and Musset, he finally quoted himself.

The boys winked at each other, and calmly prepared their books. They were safe; there would be no more Latin Grammar that day. If M. Lambin quoted his own verses, the battle was won. He wiped his brow and moved his arms to and fro according to the rhythm of the lines. His grey eyes shone with a new light and his bald head was covered with beads of perspiration. He was very hot and very happy. So were the boys.

> "Voyez la rose
> Sur laquelle l'abeille se pose
> Incline son front charmant. . . ."⁹

He did not go further. The door opened and the headmaster entered with an inspector. The boys jumped to their feet, but M. Lambin instead of greeting his visitors, stood amazed as if confronted with the head of Medusa.

"Go on, M. Lambin, do not let us disturb you," said the inspector kindly. But M. Lambin had lost the thread of his speech, he tried in vain to explain.

"That boy was asking me about the Romaunt of the Rose," he murmured, blushing to the tips of his ears.

The headmaster frowned slightly: "I thought this hour was devoted to Latin Grammar," he remarked, "at least the time-table says so."

"Quite right, sir, perfectly right."

"This seems to be a very advanced subject for children of that age, M. Lambin," observed the smiling inspector.

"Oh, yes, very advanced, sir. I should not have chosen it. In fact, they did. . . ."

"Well, well," interrupted the headmaster, "let us go back to Grammar. We are not yet in 'rhétorique'" (which is the name given to Class I, the highest of the Athénée).

The results of the subsequent examination were very poor. M. Lambin was dejected, the children were flustered, and the most appalling mistakes were made right and left.

After one of the boys had given "rosibus" as the dative plural, the inspector, who was smiling no longer, left the room somewhat abruptly, with this parting shot: "You were quite right, Monsieur le Préfet, we are not yet 'en rhétorique.'"

They both turned their back on M. Lambin who bowed again and again. He was still bowing when the door closed behind them. Then he dragged himself to his chair, dropped his head into his hands and did not utter

another word until the bell rang. At the
sound, he dismissed the boys with a wave of
his hand. They left the room silently as if
they had just witnessed a tragedy.

Pieter and Mathieu lingered behind. M.
Lambin did not notice them standing close to
him. When he heard the last pupil leaving
the room, his shoulders heaved. The poet was
sobbing. Pieter pulled gently at his sleeve.

"Do not cry, sir. It was my fault. I will
go to the headmaster and explain." M. Lambin
turned on him almost angrily:

"If you dare to go to the 'Préfet' I will keep
you here until six, do you hear? What business have you with him?"

"I thought I might explain, sir."

"Don't talk nonsense. Am I the master here
or are you?"

"You are, sir."

"Very well, then. . . . Go home and do not
think of it any longer. Neither will I. I am
only sorry I could not finish the poem. I will
recite it to you one day. Only, we will choose
a French lesson. Good-bye."

As Mathieu and Pieter reached the door, M. Lambin stopped them.

"By the way, Segers, you might bring that book of yours along one day. I should like to compare your edition with mine."

"Certainly, sir, with pleasure."

And that is why M. Lambin never left the VIIth Class, in spite of his long services. If he had only been bold enough, he could have reached the top of his profession. But he was one of those elect souls who never shine before their equals and their superiors, and who spend the best of their efforts where they cannot be rewarded.

A View of Antwerp

· V

ANTWERP

DURING the years at school, the friendship between Mathieu and Pieter widened and deepened. They had entered the world and tasted some of its hardships. Mathieu, who was rather slow at learning and who was not served by a good memory, went through many anxieties and experienced some punishments. Pieter was a great favourite with his masters but, in spite of that, or probably for that same reason, was not popular at first among his schoolfellows. An alliance established itself quite naturally between the two boys. The little Fleming helped his friend with his lessons and exercises, the sturdy Walloon helped his by protecting him against the school's professional bullies. It soon became known that whoever teased or worried Pieter would have to account for it to Mathieu, and Mathieu, in spite of his small size, spread around him a healthy respect.

Thanks to this arrangement, both boys were allowed to spend their first years at school, practically unmolested.

They had ceased by then to talk of their little differences. Their contact with strange and sometimes hostile surroundings had considerably lessened their importance. Pieter had developed a new taste for reading and spent long hours in Madame Segers's library. Mathieu, on his side, was hard at work making an herbarium. When it rained, which happens nearly every other day in Flanders during the winter months, the two boys spent their time indoors and Pieter took the lead. When they could take walks, Mathieu, a tin box slung across his shoulders, became the chief of the expedition and guided his friend through brooks and marshes in search of rare flowers.

The evening found them gathered in Marianne's kitchen or, when Pieter's mother felt well enough, in Madame Segers's room. Sometimes old Dr. Mestdagh dropped in and beamed at the result of his efforts. He used to talk it over with Marianne while warming himself at the kitchen fire and sipping the glass of hot wine which was always ready for him when he called.

"Did I not tell you that the boy needed company? Look at him now. I guess he has put on five pounds these last months. He is as sound as a horse."

"Oh! he is right enough, sir. It is only Madame who worries me now. She coughs very badly at night."

Doctor Mestdagh frowned a little, but watching the eyes of the two boys fixed upon him, he dismissed the remark lightly.

"Of course, you must worry. Marianne will always worry, my boys. If it is not one, it must be the other. What would a busy woman like Marianne do if she had nothing to worry about?"

"You know that Madame will go to see the Captain off?"

"That remains to be seen. When is he leaving?"

"Next Thursday, by the *Leopold II*. She said that we should all go together, that the boys would enjoy it."

"Why does not the Captain call here before he goes?"

"It was all settled in a hurry. He could not manage it somehow."

"I must talk it over with her. Just run upstairs and see if she is ready to see me."

Marianne hurried out of the room. Dr. Mestdagh was pulling at his pipe thoughtfully; his brow clouded ominously. Pieter feared for their plans. For a month his mother had promised him this trip to Antwerp when Uncle Dierx left for the Congo. They were talking of nothing else. They had bought a map of Africa[10] in order to follow the Captain's wanderings through the dark continent. For the first time, Geography had seemed a

most delightful science. And then there was
Antwerp with its many attractions, the Zoo, the
docks, and the ships ready to sail across the
sea. Would they have to give it up after all?

"Monsieur Mestdagh?"

"Well, my boy?"

"Do you think mother is not well enough
to go to Antwerp?"

"Look here, Pieter . . ." and he stopped short,
pulling at his pipe, "ask no questions and you
will hear no lies." Marianne had come back
and the Doctor followed her upstairs, slamming the door behind him.

"He's in a nasty temper," remarked Mathieu.

"Yes, . . . I don't know. It is the first time
he has spoken to me like that. He must be
worried by something."

"Grown-ups will always worry." The two
boys dismissed the incident and went back to
their books. They had just discovered Stanley's work and were soon absorbed gazing at
the pictures and moving in a world of virgin
forest, fierce negroes, poisoned arrows and
wild game. They did not hear Dr. Mestdagh

upstairs, having a heated argument with Madame Segers:

"I tell you, you cannot go. In your state of weakness, it would be sheer folly."

"My dear Doctor, I could not disappoint the boys."

"Now, will you listen to me or not? It is an order. I simply cannot allow you to travel in this weather. It is freezing to-night."

"Exactly, it is bound to be warmer in a week. The weather is so variable in our dear country. You will see that it will do me good. I need a change."

"If you go, I will not look after you any longer. There are plenty of doctors in Bruges."

"My dear old Mestdagh, I would not think of leaving you. By the way, what do you think of Pieter?"

"The young scoundrel is as fit as a fiddle."

"Thanks to you."

"Rubbish! Now, mind you, don't let me hear another word of this Antwerp business!"

They parted good friends, but Madame Segers never meant to give way. She thought the Doctor over-anxious and did not want to disappoint the children now that everything had been arranged.

It was a very merry party which arrived, on the following Tuesday, at the Hôtel du Grand Miroir, in the very centre of Old Antwerp, between the Place Verte and the Cathedral. The boys were very much excited by the journey and all the new things they had just seen on the road and passing through the town. They danced rather than walked at the side of their mothers, asked question after question without waiting for the answer, and enjoyed the wild intoxication of discoverer, which is certainly one of the deepest joys which human nature can experience.

Antwerp was a revelation to the two boys. The large proportions of the town, the intense traffic of its narrow streets, the hustle and bustle of the dockers in the port, the number of ships lying alongside the quays, the loading and unloading, the whistling and hooting, dazed and dazzled them. They had imagined Antwerp as a large city, twice, perhaps three times, as large as Bruges, with a stream and

some ships gliding along as they glide along
the Sluis canal; they had imagined the same
quiet life regulated by chiming bells and old
customs. And they found themselves thrown
abruptly into a devouring furnace of life and
movement. Surely, compared to this, Bruges
was asleep, Bruges was dead. They had only
to look at the rolling water of the broad stream,
too wide to be crossed by a bridge, and to think
of the stillness of the Bruges canals to realise
the change brought by their new surroundings. The Scheldt rolled towards the sea, or
towards the land, according to the tide, but
it was never still. There were ships there,
huge steamers which would have dwarfed the
largest barges. Men ran up and down steep
planks loaded with sacks and barrels like ants
around an anthill, the cobblestones rang with
the traffic of wagons. The noise was terrific.
In Bruges, one had only to whisper to make
one's self heard, here one had to shout till one
grew hoarse. It was terrible and beautiful,
at once tiring and exhilarating. Flanders was
awake and moving. No time was wasted in
vain ceremonies; people nodded to each other

and hurried on. Their accent was different,
rough and sharp. The whole town was abrupt
and imperious. No "Béguinage"[1] here, where
the old maids walk in couples under the shade
of elm trees; no long prayers in quiet churches.
Religion itself became active. There was no
time left for contemplation, all was work,
work, work. The old cathedral erected its
proud spire like a tower of strength, like a
great arm raised towards God in an eloquent
gesture of stone.

They took a small steamer and went down
stream towards the sea, as far as Lillo, and
further still, where the estuary becomes so
broad that the banks can no longer be seen.
The boat ploughed the waves caused by the
large steamers which left and entered the port
unceasingly. It was the sea, but not the deserted sea which they had pictured to themselves; a living sea alive with hundreds of
craft which obscured the sky with their smoke
and tore the air with their hooting.

They visited the Zoo, and here again the
variety of life amazed them. It seemed as
if the whole animal world had met in the

metropolis, as if every country had sent its animals to be represented in the great garden. It seemed to the children a sort of caged Eden where all the colours, all the shapes, all the cries of the Creation had been gathered together.

And, above all, from the old Place Verte, from the new docks, from the Tête de Flandre and from Lillo, the great tower of the cathedral could always be seen as the supreme expression of life. It stood there like an exclamation point at the end of a great speech. If the stones had spoken, they would not have whispered their prayer, like the stones of Bruges's great churches, they would have cried it aloud.

To go from Bruges to Antwerp is to awake from sleep, to pass from a world of dreams and mystery to a world of stern and moving reality, from a kingdom of calm and silence to an empire of hustle and noise. The material horizon of Bruges is limited by the walls of the town. Antwerp's forts are too far from the centre to be noticed; they are merely incidents in the surrounding landscape. Through

its huge western door, gilded by the setting
sun, through the wide rolling Scheldt, the
great port receives its life. This door opens
on the sea, on the world; it is the way to palm
trees and icebergs, white Bedouins and dirty
Esquimaux, scented flowers and green parrots,
the way trodden by all adventurers from Gul-
liver to Robinson Crusoe and from Stanley to
Captain Dierx.

They saw him off next day. He came to
fetch them at the hôtel du Grand Miroir. He
was as abrupt and alert as ever, but Pieter
was impressed by the gravity of his manner.
While he was looking through the window, in
the hotel's sitting room, he heard his mother
whisper:

"When do you intend to come back, dear?"

"In two years if my work is over by then."

"Surely it cannot last so long."

"It is impossible to tell."

"At least, promise to come back at the end
of your engagement."

"I cannot promise that."

"It is not only for you, dear. Think of
the boy. If anything happened to me——"

"Nonsense."

"Remember what Dr. Mestdagh told you last year. . . . I do not like to think of you so far, out of reach, in danger perhaps. . . ."

"You forget that I am a soldier. If I were married, I should have to leave my wife and my own children just as I am leaving you and the boy."

"Surely, you would never do that!"

"What is the use of remaining here when there is nothing to do?"

"But what is the Congo to you? Surely these native risings are none of your business?"

"It is my country's business."

"Are you sure of that?"

"My dear girl, you are a great deal too fond of reasoning. Let everybody do his job. The country is in for it. The least I can do is to serve her."

Pieter was very uncomfortable. While discussing, they had raised their voices and, though he felt he ought not to have listened, he could not help hearing every word. He finally jumped from the chair where he was

kneeling and walked out of the room. He had
a lump in his throat and his eyes were burning. Two years before, he would have rushed
to Marianne and told her his trouble. But
school-life had already strengthened his en-
ergy. He kept his own counsel and decided to
talk it over with Mathieu, later on. In the
meantime, he wondered at the meaning of his
mother's words. What could happen to her?
And above all, what was this new feeling which
possessed Uncle Dierx? What was the meaning of this word "country," of this mysterious
power to which all natural affections must be
sacrificed. He was very angry with the Captain for not giving way, and, at the same time,
he could not help admiring him all the more
for it. But the whole thing was dreadful. He
felt as if he stood at the edge of a precipice
whose existence he had not suspected before.
The school-world which had seemed so large
after the quiet life at home was dwarfed by
this glimpse of real life. For a few hours, he
was made miserable and restless. But the
atmosphere cleared when they boarded the
Leopold II.

It was the first large steamer on board of
which the boys had been and everything was
new and wonderful to them, from the wide
funnels to the engine-room. Mathieu was
especially eager and led the way lower and
lower in the mysterious vitals of the ship,
when they were stopped by a grimy stoker who
sent them flying back to the deck.

The passengers, surrounded by their friends
and relatives, were scattered about in small
groups. The sun was bright, but a bleak De-
cember wind whistled through the rigging and
rocked the steamer like a huge cradle. Some
women sobbed; from time to time, a man tried
to raise a laugh which soon fizzled out. Captain Dierx strolled calmly up and down at the
side of his sister. She was seized with a bad
fit of coughing and Marianne hurried to her
and wrapped her in a shawl in spite of her
protests. The Captain smiled:

"That's right, Marianne! You look after
her when I am away. I leave her to you."

"That's all very well, sir, but she will not
listen to me. If she had listened, she would
not be here to-day."

At that moment, the Captain saw the two boys appearing on the deck and signalled to them. He seized Pieter by the scruff of his neck and shook him lightly:

"Now, where have you been, young rascal. I am afraid you two will give a lot of trouble to your mothers. Now, mind you, don't let me hear anything against you when I come back, otherwise . . ." and he rolled his eyes and frowned threateningly. The boys roared with delight. It was at this moment that the whistle sounded and the military band, on the quay, began to play. The Captain clasped his sister in his arms.

"Mind you, look after yourself, no more foolish pranks while I am away. Farewell, dear, God bless you!"

They were the last to leave the boat and join the crowd lining the quay. The band had struck up the "Brabançonne."[1] Women nodded and waved around them. Pieter watched the face of his mother who had turned suddenly very pale and shivered in her fur coat. She had put her handkerchief to her lips and a bright tear rolled down her

Peter felt Mathieu's hand seizing his.

cheek. The Captain stood at the stern while
the ship was gathering speed. He did not
smile, merely looked at them intently and once
raised his hand for a last military salute.
Further and further went the ship bound for
a strange land, a strange climate, strange
tropical races, which nevertheless were part of
this small Kingdom in the North. A long
streak of smoke floated behind the *Leopold
II.* The straight figure of the Captain was
scarcely visible. But those who were borne
away must still have heard the strains of the
"Brabançonne" carried to them by the bleak
east wind.

Pieter felt Mathieu's hand seizing his. His
friend was biting his lip, his eyes fixed on the
distant spot, the flowing streak of smoke
against the horizon.

Was he also sad that Uncle Dierx had left
for so long, or did he feel, for the first time,
that love of country which was to be the greatest passion of his life?

The Flemish Plain

VI

IN THE TRAIN

More than a year later, our two friends are seated in the express train from Ostend to Brussels and Arlon, on their way to the Ardennes.

Marianne has placed the boys near the window. Mathieu is sitting facing the engine, the breeze ruffling his hair. Pieter is opposite, looking paler and more serious than before. He wears a crêpe band on his left arm and, while the familiar landscape of the Flemish plain glides before his eyes, he thinks of all that has happened since we left him on the quay at Antwerp while the band played the "Brabançonne."

This journey brings it home to him more than anything else: he is leaving Bruges for good. It is not for a holiday. He will perhaps never come back. And if he came back and rang the bell of the dear old house, on the Quai du Rosaire, some stranger would open the door. It is all so near and so far already. Still, some images remain, the darkest of his life. At their return from Antwerp, his mother took to her bed. Old Mestdagh came every day for months and, during the last weeks, he scarcely left the house. At their return from school, the boys were not allowed upstairs and they were told to be very quiet. Long conferences followed between the Doctor and Marianne and Pieter's mother coughed, oh, how she coughed! When, from time to time, he was shown into her bedroom, he found her breathing heavily, her eyes very bright. He felt her burning kisses on his forehead and, when the short time allowed was up, she was loth to let him go from her.

At first, he was so absorbed with his school

life and his games that he did not understand
that anything unusual had happened. He was
accustomed to see his mother ill. One day,
he found Marianne weeping into her apron in
a corner of the kitchen, just as she had wept
for little Annette. But, when he asked what
had happened, she only sobbed more bitterly
and shook her head in despair. Then he
questioned old Mestdagh, who rebuked him
gruffly, muttering something about spoiled
children and the stupidity of women in general
and mothers in particular. Another day, as
he came from school, he saw the old priest of
the neighbouring church leaving the house.
He ran after him; but he also would not
speak, only looked at him kindly and patted
him on the shoulder. He felt more and more
uncomfortable as he noticed the pity of all
those he met.

Mathieu was his only comfort. When the
shock came at last and he realized that all was
over, he ran to the bottom of the garden
where his friend was digging. He felt that
his heart would burst if he could not cry out
his despair. But Mathieu understood him be-

fore he spoke. He calmly let his spade fall
on the path and, putting his arm round Pieter's
shoulders, he sat with him on the green wooden
bench against the hedge. He held him very
tight, much tighter than he had ever held
him before, and begged him to be brave and
stand it like a man: "You must do it for her,
you see, you must show her that you do not
despair. She will see you from where she is
and feel happier about it."

Some people may argue that the happy
spirits cannot be happier than they are and
are no longer interested in our earthly troubles.
But no child will ever believe it. Mathieu's
words were the only ones which could bring
a little strength to his friend. He might have
been right or wrong, I do not know, but he
helped his companion in the bitterest hour of
his life, and it does not seem that you can be
very wrong when you do so much good.

As he was sitting there in the railway carriage, listening to the tick-a-tack of the train
and following abstractedly the telegraph wires
rising and falling abruptly when they reached
a pole, Pieter still felt his mother's burning kiss

on his brow, he still saw her parting look, but he felt also the steady pressure of his friend's arm around his shoulders and heard him whisper: "Be a man Pieter, be a man for her sake." The tears rose again to his eyes, but he controlled himself, biting his lip and looking at Mathieu and Marianne sitting opposite.

Marianne, in spite of the hard bench of the third-class carriage, was slowly rocked to sleep by the movement of the train. She leaned sometimes on the left, on Mathieu's shoulder, sometimes on the right on that of a fat Flemish farmer, who sat as stiff as a poker, anxious not to crease his best Sunday clothes. Poor Marianne, she had spent the night packing. There was not much to pack, only their three trunks, but there was a great deal of sorting to do, there were many souvenirs and letters to burn or to take away—things which could not be profaned by a public sale.

As the proverb goes "Un malheur n'arrive jamais seul" (misfortunes never come singly), Almost at the same time that Madame Segers's soul had left the quiet house of the Quai du

Rosaire for still serener regions, her lawyer
and adviser who had managed all her business
matters and into whose hands she had trusted
her little fortune, had failed suddenly and fled
to Greece. So that, within a few days, the
boy had been left a ruined orphan without any
relatives to look after him. Without relatives
but not without friends. Dr. Mestdagh had
spoken of adopting the child, but Marianne
would not hear of it: "Mathieu and Pieter
were brothers when he was rich, they will remain brothers now. Madame may rest in
peace." She had even refused the doctor's kind
offer of money, saying that her father's farm
was large enough for them all and that "if
there was enough for four, there should be
enough for five."

In his deep misery, Pieter had scarcely realized what happened. He was much too fond
of Marianne to be very grateful to her. He
took his adoption as a matter of course. He
did not even mind leaving Bruges for a time
and, in any other circumstances, the prospect
of going with Mathieu to the Ardennes would
have filled him with joy. Only he would have

liked to leave the old house as it was before
and think that, later on, he could come back
to it.   This new separation revived the pain
of the other one.   It was losing his mother
twice to be torn from the country in which he
had lived at her side such happy years.

The train slowed down and stopped somewhat abruptly.   Marianne woke with a start.

"Is that Brussels already?"

"No, only Ghent," muttered the farmer who
was busy unlocking the door.

"Ghent?   What a pity we cannot stop!   Do
you remember Ghent, Pieter?"

Yes, Pieter remembered.   He had been there
some years before to meet Uncle Dierx, and
he explained to Mathieu that it was very much
like Bruges only less beautiful and more alive.
There was a belfry, and canals, and a great
Church called St. Bavon where he remembered
seeing a wonderful picture.

"What was it like?"

"It is rather difficult to explain.   You just
imagine a huge meadow full of flowers, like
in a dream.   In the centre, is a lamb standing

on a sort of table or altar and all round you
see saints and angels worshipping."

"What is it all about?"

"I suppose it is a picture of Paradise. At
least that is how I imagine things should be
over there."

Mathieu did not insist any further. He had
some doubts about the possibility of painting
the Unseen but he kept them wisely to himself.
Many years later, when he was able to see the
masterpiece of Van Eyck, he remembered
Pieter's enthusiasm and understood it better.

The country outside was rather monotonous.
For miles and miles, the same meadows, the
same fields green with the young crops, the
same rows of poplars, the same winding
streams, the same pollard willows whose spring
shoots looked yellow and reddish against the
bright blue sky, the same red-tiled, white-
washed cottages scattered in the plain with
their green shutters and the neat patches of
multicoloured sand before their green doors.
Flanders ought never to be looked at from a
train; her beauty is in the light and in the

thousand details of the landscape. It cannot be perceived at a glance.

"Look, Pieter, a hill!" They were nearing Brussels, and Mathieu, who was watching eagerly for the first change, pointed to a slight rising of the ground. It was scarcely perceptible, but, as they were going south the streams appeared to sink more and more between low ridges and the lanes between their banks. They saw the same trees, the same fields but the flat monotony of the plain was broken. With a pang, Pieter realized that they had left Flanders and reached Brabant.

They did not alight in Brussels. After stopping at the North Station, their train took them round the outskirts of the capital through a very commonplace quarter to the Station du Luxembourg whence they started for Namur.

It was for Pieter a very exciting experience, and he forgot his trouble for a time. Marianne had unpacked their luncheons and the two boys, eating and chatting gaily, on both sides of the window, were entirely absorbed by the journey. The sun shone brightly and in the *forêt de Soignes,* which they were crossing, the first touches of green appeared on the bushes. There was a strong feeling of spring in the air. Near Groenendael, they saw a deer galloping under the beeches, the high beeches whose trunks show like columns of green marble. The passengers who entered at the next station were talking with Mathieu's singing accent and, as some of them addressed Marianne and she answered them in their patois, Pieter felt faintly as if he were a stranger in his own country.

The manners of the people they met were also very different from what he was used to see at Bruges. Accustomed to the shy reserve of the Flemings, the boy could not understand at first how they could chaff each other without quarrelling, and laugh so heartily when he could not discover any reason for merriment.

"La Meuse, La Meuse!" They were crossing the Great Walloon stream on an iron bridge. In the distance, Pieter saw the outlines of the old fortress of Namur. The Meuse was not so large as the Scheldt at Antwerp but, as Mathieu explained, it had still a long way to go before reaching the sea:

Liége and Maestricht and Holland, "and then,
there are the hills!"

This remark seemed to explain everything.
For everything had changed since Brussels.
They had not seen a windmill for hours, the
only mills they met were water-mills. The
roads were no longer straight and paved with
cobblestones, but winding up and down hill and
covered with macadam. The blue slate had
taken the place of the red tile on the roofs,
and the rough stones had superseded the
bricks on the walls. There were no willows
left, scarcely any poplars, but long rows of
pine trees and rowan-trees along the roads.
Some rocks actually pierced through the mantle
of heather, broom and brushwood which grew
on the sides of the valleys, where clear shal-
low trout streams rushed along among the
stones. It was indeed another country fresh
and cheery in the spring sun. The air itself
was different, colder and bracing. The first
words of Mathieu when they alighted at Poix
were:

"Smell, Pieter, smell the Ardennes!"

Pieter perceived a strange scent made of

burnt wood and smoked bacon which pervaded the village. And this scent conveyed to him better perhaps than anything else the change which had occurred in his life. In the steam tram for St. Hubert, every turn of the road was a fresh surprise.

"Will Annette be at the station?" asked Mathieu.

"Yes," answered Marianne. "Grandfather promised me to take her if it was fine."

Annette? Grandfather? Pieter had forgotten, in the excitement of the journey, that there were some more surprises in store for him. He felt somewhat uneasy about Grandfather. Several things which he had heard had made him realize that he was sometimes bad-tempered and self-willed. He pulled Marianne's arm.

"Marianne?"

"Yes, dear."

"Did you tell him that I was coming?"

"Of course, I told him."

"And . . . do you think he will be angry?"

"Angry? I should think not! Why should he be angry? He may have us, the three of

us, or none at all. Did I not promise Madame
to look after you?"

With that energetic reply, the tram stopped
at the foot of the hill on the top of which is
built the large church, dedicated to Hubert,
patron saint of hunters, in the heart of the
Ardennes. The two boys were first to jump
out of the carriage. While they were reliev-
ing Marianne of her parcels they heard a deep
voice behind them:

"There you are, there you are at last!
That's a good thing!" And a large grey-
bearded fellow with a straw hat, holding his
whip in his hand, leaned forward towards
Marianne, nearly upsetting Pieter. He lifted
Mathieu and kissed him on both cheeks, laughing, chatting and answering his own questions.

"There you are, sonny! And what's the
matter with you? All right? That's a good
thing! Still a true Walloon, eh? Not got the
Flemish disease? I should think not, sonny
of mine." But Marianne interrupted him:

"This is Pieter Segers," she said firmly, but
somewhat timidly, pushing Pieter towards the
old man.

His face changed suddenly. He grinned awkwardly, took off his hat, scratched his shaggy head and, as Pieter was trying to shake hands, he pinched his ear with a sour smile.

"Yes, a true Fleming; well, it would be the first time that I should get on with a Fleming! Never mind, I will not be your nurse. I understand Marianne does that. Though, at your age, my boy, I was already earning my bread and cheese in keeping the village flock. Still, I suppose *you* are too clever to do such a thing. So, don't let us talk of it any longer."

And, without heeding Marianne's indignant protest, he led the way towards a small trap which was waiting for them outside.

Pieter was rather taken aback at first, but his attention was now attracted by a girl who stood on the seat of the trap. "There is our brother Pieter!" cried Mathieu as soon as he saw her. She had extraordinary blue eyes. "Blue as a Flemish sky, at sunset," thought Pieter. And the smile of these eyes made him forget entirely the strange greeting he had received from Grandfather.

La Roche

VII

"THE THREE FIRS"

GRANDFATHER'S farm, the "Three Firs,"
was situated on a by-road, about two miles
from St. Hubert, in the direction of La Roche.
It lay alone on the top of a hill, in the midst
of a clearing. Towards the north, the view
was shut in by the woods; but towards the
south, one could see miles away over the
Ourthe valley. Wooded hill succeeded wooded
hill, wave of forest succeeded wave of forest,
as the winding river disappeared in the distance and, since no house could be seen, the
place seemed an oasis of fields in a desert of

trees. On the ridge, just above the roof of the house, stood the three mighty fir trees which had given its name to the farm. Between two of them, was an old wooden crucifix bent by the winter gales.

It was a typical farmstead of the Ardennes, built of rough grey stones, the large overhanging roof of the house being covered with blue slates, while the stables were roofed with a dark old thatch with bright patches of moss and grass. The gate was in a dilapidated condition and the outside wall was in ruin. The first thing that struck you when you entered the yard was a huge dung hill, in the centre, and a duck pond, around which the poultry assembled all the day long. One side of the square was taken by the stables, the other by the barn and sheds, the third, in the centre, by the dwelling house. There was always something or other happening in the yard: the ducks squabbled, the cock crowed defiance, the geese trotted along like a troop of loud-voiced, frightened old maids, a cow lowed in the stable, a labourer strolled to his work, walking heavily. But the moment you passed outside the iron gate, silence took hold of you, a silence more solemn and more awe inspiring than the mysterious quietude of any dream-town. There was scarcely any traffic on the small by-road, for it led only, beyond the farm, to a few vague tracks through the forest, the fields and pastures. "The Three Firs" stood as a light patch of green in the midst of dark stretches covered with beeches, which spread around it for miles on every side.

While Mathieu took up farm work at once, Marianne had arranged that Pieter should take a holiday until the next autumn, when she hoped to send him to school somewhere. Her plans were somewhat vague and she very likely lacked the means of putting them into execution, but she felt strongly that Pieter was not made for farm work and that he ought to finish his studies. Grandfather submitted with a sour smile: "Go ahead, my girl," he said, "if you want the boy to be a good-for-nothing he will become one soon enough. But, if later you send him back to school, don't come and ask my help. What was good enough for me, what is good enough for Mathieu, is good enough for him."

Pieter had come to realize that he was an unwelcome guest at "The Three Firs." He tried at first to help Mathieu in his work, but he was very clumsy with his hands, and so afraid of being jeered at by the farm-labourers that he soon gave up the attempt. He was fifteen now, but naturally weak for his age and, in his zeal, made the mistake of undertaking things above his strength. One day, while carrying jars of milk to the dairy, he stumbled and fell in front of the house upsetting them. Another day, having been sent to carry an urgent message to St. Hubert, he tried a short cut, lost himself in the wood and, when he arrived at last, the farmer who had been waiting for him had already left. As bad luck would have it, Grandfather was always the first to hear of any of these mishaps and made the most of them. "That boy of yours, Marianne, will make our fortune. If he goes on like that, I shall give up farming and buy a house in town. He is a find, that little Fleming is, clever and skillful and quick-

witted! Really you are quite right about him.
He is too good for this kind of work. Far
too good! Don't you think it is about time he
should give it up?"

Marianne, of course, protested violently,
taking Pieter's part, and Mathieu spoke also
for his friend, but the obstinate old man would
hear nobody. "Have your own way, have your
own way, I don't mind. As long as he does
not interfere with my work, it will be all right.
He is here for a holiday, I understand; very
well then, let it be as short as possible. I
don't want any loafer in this place!"

With these words, he turned his back on
them. His voice could be heard in the fields
far away, as he was spending his bad temper
on the two farm-servants. Grandfather was
a hard master, but they liked him all the same
because, according to their own words, "he
understood a joke."

Pieter had always been touchy and sensitive.
The loss of his mother, the change of circumstances had still further increased this self-
consciousness. He felt desperately lonely and
miserable. Since he could no longer work on

the farm, he saw very little of Mathieu who was kept busy all day long. He felt so depressed that he had even ceased to confide in his friend. His only comfort, when it was fine, was to take one of his books into the woods and read under the shade of the trees. He had first chosen the group of great fir trees, close to the house, but he soon left that spot, as Grandfather passed often this way and never lost an opportunity of teasing him. The old man despised intellectual work. He shared the peasants' scorn for anything which is not connected with the soil: "There you are again, Pieter Segers," he used to say, "sitting under your tree like King Louis; well, what have you learned to-day? Can you tell me if next month will be fine, or if I must sow oats or wheat in the next field? You can not? I thought so. Then, what is the use of all your books and reading?" And he went on without waiting for an answer, while the boy, flushed and angry, shut his book and fled to the woods to find a sheltered corner where he could read in peace.

A great bitterness grew in Pieter's heart.

"Whatever I do," he thought, "I will do wrong
for him. If I work, I am a fool; if I read I
am lazy. Marianne and Mathieu are made
wretched on my account. They would be happier if I went away. I am not wanted here."
And he began to think of leaving the farm
for good. But an incident detained him.

As he was leaning, one bright spring afternoon, against the smooth trunk of a beech,
in the midst of a clearing, he heard the crackling of dry branches. Thinking that it was
a deer, he kept very quiet. He had learned
to watch the game and knew that, if the wind
blew in the right direction and if you did not
stir, the most timid beast would sometimes
come quite close, moved by curiosity. So he
kept still, his eyes only moving right and left
in order to catch sight of the intruder. But
the faint crackling and rustling came now
from behind the beech; it crept closer and
closer. It seemed to him that he could hear
the beast breathing; then, suddenly, two hands
closed on his eyes and he heard the familiar
laughter of Annette: "Guess now, guess now,
who is it?"

"A little fawn?"

"No!"

"An imp of the woods?"

"No!"

"Well, then, Annetteke?"

"Yes!"

It is the inveterate habit of the Flemings to add *ke* to the names of those they are fond of, whether these names are Flemish or not; and, from the first days of their acquaintance, Pieter had invented this pet-name for his new friend. He was very fond of it because he was the only one to use it.

"What are you doing here?"

"Reading."

"And I have been gathering daffodils. Look!" And she showed the boy a large bunch in her apron. It gleamed like a patch of sun in the dark wood.

"Where did you find them?"

"There below, along the brook. Will you come and help me to gather some more? Or do you prefer to go on reading?"

"I am tired of reading."

"Why do you do it then?"

"Because there is nothing else to do."

And, as they strolled among the trees, Pieter confided in Annette. Her large blue eyes were frequently turned towards his. Each time he stopped talking, a fresh look from Annette prompted another confession. And that was how she heard the whole sad story: The death of Madame Segers, the ruin of the family, Grandfather's hostility and the uncertainty with regard to the future. One thing only the boy did not tell: his project of leaving the farm—not because he wanted to keep it from her but because Annette had taken his hand and he felt that he would never have the courage to leave her now.

The buds of the beeches were only half open and showed grey against the blue sky, but many green and yellow patches lightened the thicket. Young shoots pierced the dead leaves at their feet and the chaffinches sang on every branch. As they stood, hand in hand, on the bank of the rushing brook, before the bright field of daffodils, the smell of spring filled Pieter's nostrils and his blood ran faster.

Annette was wearing a sun bonnet white

with pink flowers, which hid her face from the boy.

"Are you still very unhappy?" she asked in a soft voice, bending her head.

"I am not unhappy now."

"Why?"

"Because you are so kind to me and I may tell you my trouble."

Then suddenly, the little head with the brown locks turned towards him, and Pieter noticed that Annette's face was working. She was trying hard not to cry:

"I wish you would always trust me, as you did to-day. Perhaps I could be of some help to you. I am very sorry for you, dear, dear Pieter," and her small fingers clung to his. "Shall we not be friends?"

"We are friends already, Annetteke!"

The ridiculous name awakened her laughter. She left his hand, sprang lightly over the brook and began to gather the flowers, singing one of her familiar songs:

> "Dans l'jardin d'mon père[13]
> Un oiseau il y a,
> Un oiseau, à la volette,
> Un oiseau, à la volette,
> Un oiseau il y a."

Pieter leaned heavily against a tree. He was dazed with joy. It seemed to him, that since his mother's death he had lived in the dark, and now he was suddenly brought out of his cell into the full sun of springtime. His heart was thumping in his breast. Surely, it was good to live. He breathed the smell of the moss and of the dead leaves, he looked round as if discovering for the first time the magic beauty of the woods through which he had strolled so many times without heeding them, but his eyes came back always to the young girl, in her white sunbonnet, gathering the bright yellow flowers like so many rays of sun. The dear, trembling voice went on:

> "Il dit tous les jours
> Qu'il s'envolera
> Qu'il s'envole—à la volette,
> Qu'il s'envole—à la volette,
> Qu'il s'envolera."

And it seemed to him that he would give the last drop of blood in his veins for his new friend; that the devotion of a whole life could not repay her for her pity. Yes, if it only depended on him, her clear blue eyes should

never shed a tear, and her dear unsteady voice
should never cease singing:

> "L'bel oiseau s'envole
> Sur un chêne au bois,
> Sur un chêne—à la volette,
> Sur un chêne—à la volette,
> Sur un chêne au bois."

The Road to St. Hubert

VIII

ALONE

THESE were indeed happy days. Summer was coming fast and the two children had every opportunity of meeting and roaming through the woods together. Grandfather, who was devoted to Annette, never allowed her in the farm or dairy. So that, when she had helped Marianne with the household work, she was at liberty to do what she liked.

Pieter accompanied Annette everywhere. One day, they went in the woods to pick strawberries or raspberries, another, they sat and

read together in the shade. Pieter was in-
structed in woodlore, he learned to distinguish
the birds, the flowers and the trees and to
watch the ways of insects. Nature was new
to him; he admired it without understanding.
Annette taught him what she knew. It was
not much, but it was quite enough to enlarge
his outlook on life. The boy was by now de-
veloping fast into a man. He had lived until
then in a hothouse, in his mother's bedroom,
in the narrow streets and the narrow ways of
Bruges, with only one or two glances at the
outside world. The Flemish country-side, too
cultivated, too thickly populated, could not open
his eyes to the splendour of the wilds. Annette took him to the top of the moor and into
the depth of the valley, along tracks which
only the wood-cutters and the keepers knew.
It was easy to imagine that no one had ever
been there before, that they were discovering
a new world, and they laughed sometimes,
thinking of Adam and Eve in the garden of
Eden.

Pieter began to realize that man was not
alone on earth, that human life was only the

supreme expression of unconscious hidden
forces. And that all man's efforts and long-
ings were, as it were, painted on a background
where beasts, plants and rocks found their
natural place. There came into his mind a
certain sense of proportion which steadied his
otherwise over-sensitive character. He knew
only too well how much he was to himself;
he had still to learn how little he mattered in
the eyes of Mother Earth.

"I suppose," he said once to Annette, "I
suppose that all Belgium is scarcely more than
a large ant-hill and we two are like two ants
running over it."

"Yes," said Annette, pensively, "two ants
with eternal souls and God to look after them."

Annette was very devout, like most peasants
of the Ardennes valleys.

When they began to read, Pieter became the
teacher. He showed his books to Annette with
a boyish pride. He had a true instinct for
poetry and read to her some verses by Lamar-
tine, Hugo and Musset out of an Anthology,
a prize-book given to him the year before.
Annette did not always understand the mean-

ing of every word, but the drift and harmony of the poems were clear enough. She used to listen to them lying on her back, her eyes closed, her arms folded under her head. She never interrupted. She merely lifted her head, from time to time, whispering "Thank you, Pieter, go on." And he went on until the sun set behind the trees and they heard a distant church-bell urging them back to the farm.

Then they got up and, hand in hand, climbed down the steep hill towards the "Three Firs." They had never referred to their former conversation. They both felt so happy together that they did not want even to say so. They enjoyed the present too much to speak of the past or the future. Their friendship was an understood thing. No promise could have strengthened it.

Life at home was not so happy. When, at meal times, the whole family was gathered round the table, a cloud seemed to weigh upon them. Marianne had lost her bright manners. She no longer fussed anxiously over the children. She went about her work slow-footed and frowning. Mathieu's ways also

were changed. He looked worried and scarcely
spoke to Pieter and Annette. As for Grandfather, he no longer teased "the little Fleming"
but, whenever he looked at him, his small grey
eyes glittered ominously. Pieter and Annette
were too much absorbed in each other to
notice these changes. They lived without care,
without anxiety, and hurried over their meals
in order to be sooner at liberty to wander
through the woods together.

One day, after dinner,—which in the Belgian
countryside is eaten in the middle of the day,
—as Pieter was taking his hat in the hall,
hurrying in order to join Annette in the yard,
he was stopped by Mathieu who asked him to
follow him into the stable.

"I want you to promise me something,
Pieter," he said, in an anxious tone.

"What can it be?"

"Whatever happens, promise me not to leave
the farm without telling me."

"But I have no intention of leaving the
farm."

"I know. But I want to make doubly sure."

"All right, my dear fellow. I should certainly not decide anything without consulting you."

"That's right. Good-bye!"

And Mathieu went to his work with a deep sigh, whilst Pieter ran out to meet Annette:

"What did Mathieu tell you?" she asked. "He looks so secretive for the last few days. I wonder what is the matter with them all."

"Oh, nothing, he only wanted to show me the new calf."

Pieter blushed to the tips of his ears, but Annette did not notice it as, at the same moment, a lark rose under her feet and she began to search for its nest. It was a wonderful afternoon. A storm had washed the dust from the trees the day before, and huge white clouds were racing through the sky. The two had scarcely reached the woods when they spied a small herd of hinds grazing in a clearing. They began to watch them and followed them through the bracken in order to see their fawns. This led them so far that they were late for supper. The others had already finished their meal. Mathieu had gone to bed, as he had to start to work very early the next

day, and Grandfather was smoking his pipe
sullenly, near the fire. He did not even greet
Annette when she entered. Marianne seemed
very depressed; her eyes were red and swollen.

"What is the matter with you, mother,"
asked Annette after explaining why they were
late.

"Nothing, child, nothing. Only a headache."

They ate their supper in silence and retired
immediately. Instead of going straight to bed,
as he was used to do after a long walk, Pieter
went into the parlour where he had left a few
books. The lamp was burning and, as he happened to open one of his favorite books, he began to read. Suddenly, he heard loud talking
in the next room. It was Grandfather's voice.
He seemed angry. . . . Were they speaking of
him? Surely he had heard his name. . . . He
listened, his heart in his throat, numb with
anxiety:

"I have had enough of it, I say. This Fleming of yours, this wretched good-for-nothing
is going to break up our family. Why have
you brought this stranger under my roof?
What right had you to adopt him? What

money can you use to bring him up? Not mine, you bet!"

"I am not asking for it." This was the voice of Marianne.

"No, but, since you have not a penny of your own and since he is as poor as a beggar, you will keep him here, under my roof. He has poisoned my life long enough. Send him away!"

"You are hard, father."

"I don't know if I am hard. I only know that I will not go on feeding a good-for-nothing who is of no use to me and who has succeeded in estranging you all from me. First you, then Mathieu, now the girl. She did not even greet me when they came back!"

"I beg your pardon, it was you who did not answer."

Grandfather's fist struck the table so violently that the glasses clinked together.

"Are you going to contradict me now? I know what I am speaking about. He has taken the affection of the girl. Only watch them together. She dotes on him. What

she can find in that flaxy, wizened-looking
creature, God only knows! But there it is."

"Why should they not be friends?"

"I am not going to discuss the matter any
further. My patience is at an end. I have
put up with him long enough."

"But what can I do?"

"Send him away."

"I have nowhere to send him."

"Find out his uncle or this precious Doctor
in Bruges, or anybody. Let him go back to
Bruges, to Brussels, or to Hell!"

"I trusted you. I told everybody that I
should take charge of him. I should never dare
to go back on my word. Remember, you
promised. . . ."

"I did not promise anything. I wrote to
you that you were all welcome under my roof.
You took too much for granted. I did not
expect that I should shelter an enemy."

"But he is not your enemy. He has done
his best to please you."

The old man broke out in loud laughter.

"His best! my congratulations! If that is
the way he sets to work to conciliate people,

I wish him good luck! He has embittered
every hour, every minute of my life since he
entered my door. That is enough. If you do
not manage to clear him out of this house
before a week is over, I will do the thing
myself."

"I forbid you. . . ."

"You . . . you. . . . Who is the master here?"

Marianne broke into loud sobs, while the
old man stamped and fumed about the room,
breaking a glass, upsetting a chair, cursing and
swearing.

Pieter got up. He felt a cold hand gripping
his heart. He winced with pain. He went to
the parlour door. He wanted to tell them that
he was going. But, as his hand was on the
latch, he heard Grandfather stop abruptly.

"What are you doing here?" he thundered.

"I heard you from my room." It was
Mathieu's calm and steady voice, the voice of
a man.

"Go back to bed. You are not wanted
here."

"I beg your pardon. I am no longer a child.

Come, mother. I will speak to Grandfather.
Perhaps he will listen to me."

"I won't. It has nothing to do with you."

"I am sorry, but this discussion must come
to an end. Since father is no longer here, it
is for me to look after Maman. She must not
be made miserable."

"Let her give up the boy. I will not say
another word."

"You know perfectly well that it is out of
the question. We must remain together. He
belongs to the family."

"What do you mean?"

"That if he goes, we must all go with him."

"You dare say that to me, in my house?"

"Certainly."

"Go, then," shrieked the old man in a broken
voice, "go, then, all of you. But don't let me
hear you, don't let me see you. I'd rather be
alone than with an enemy under my roof. But
you had better be careful. If you go . . . you
never come back. You understand? You
understand? . . ."

There was a strange appeal in the broken
voice. The door shut and Pieter heard Mari-

anne and Mathieu going upstairs. For some
time all remained still in the next room. Then
he heard that Grandfather was sobbing:
"Alone, alone, oh! my little Annette!"

He crept upstairs, wrote a short letter to
Mathieu, arranged a bunch of flowers which
he had gathered that day, tied it with a string,
and stuck in it a piece of paper on which he
wrote with a trembling hand:

"To Annetteke. In everlasting remembrance."

Then, gathering his few belongings in a
parcel, he went downstairs stealthily. He laid
the flowers before Annette's door and slipped
the letter under Mathieu's. He had taken off
his heavy nailed boots in order not to be heard.
He slipped them on in the yard sitting on a
wheelbarrow. The moon was shining and he
saw distinctly the blind of Annette's window
move in the soft summer breeze. Should she
appear like Juliet at her balcony? Oh! for a
last farewell. He had not even kissed her
cheek. . . .

As he was walking on the narrow by-road
he thought of Mathieu again and of poor

He saw the shade of Annette's window move in the summer
breeze.

Marianne. He heard the choked voice of Grandfather: "Alone, alone." And it awoke a strange echo in his heart. Had he not passed, a few hours ago, along the same road, holding Annette's little hand? He was going back with her to meet Marianne and Mathieu. His life was full and happy. A few words heard through a closed door had wrecked all his hopes. Indeed, he was alone in the night, with the summer breeze drying his tears on his cheeks and the moon shining in his face.

A year ago, he would have sat on the next milestone and cried in despair. But life had already made a man of him and with the sweet remembrance of Annette's laughter in his ears and with the burning parting kiss of his mother on his brow, he walked briskly, waving his stick. When he reached the road he turned his back to the moon and descended the hill towards St. Hubert. And the shadow walking before him was his only companion.

*Panorama of
Brussels*

IX

BRUSSELS

Pieter took three months to get to Brussels.
He went there as a moth goes to the light, as
every stray dog goes to the market place. He
had a vague hope of feeling less lonely in a
great town. Bruges had failed him, the country had failed him, perhaps Brussels would
be kinder. There were books there, public
libraries, schools, museums. He could perhaps
try to forget.

In his hurry, he had only taken with him
the few francs which Marianne had given him,
some time ago, for his pocket-money. It would

not have paid his fare to Namur. So he took
to the road and tramped. He slept in sheds
and barns, when he was lucky enough to meet
hospitable people, and in some haystack or in
some wood, when he was rebuked as a "vaga-
bond" and sent about his business. It was a
rough experience for the once pampered little
Pieter. But, on the whole, he stood it well.
When he arrived near Namur, having spent all
his money, he worked for a farmer, haymak-
ing, during a fortnight, and was rewarded with
a ten-franc piece. By then he was already so
accustomed to his new life that he did not
think of taking the train. He wanted to save
all he could in order not to arrive in Brussels
penniless. Happily the summer was very dry
and very warm and the police were not in-
quisitive. The boy was allowed to roam about
freely and his quiet manners did not awake
suspicion. When he was asked where he was
going, he said that he was on his way to Brussels in the hope of joining an uncle of his who
was coming back from the Congo. This was
partly true, for the memory of Uncle Dierx had
remained vivid in his mind. Everybody was so

busy that they did not take the trouble to inquire any further. Never did the Belgian
fields prove so generous. The ears in the corn-
fields were already heavy and, as Pieter passed
through them at noon, he smelt the character-
istic smell of baked bread, so promising to the
farmer. The peasants he met on the road
looked tired and happy. This year, 1914,
promised to be a record year for hay and corn.
The potatoes ought to do well also. It was
a good thing to be alive after all.

Pieter was still too young to feel utterly
depressed. He was sometimes very miserable
and, especially at night, when he was made
welcome at a peasant's table, a lump came into
his throat as he remembered the happy even-
ings he had spent at Bruges between his
mother and Marianne. He thought of Mathieu
also, and still more of Annette. What were
they doing now? Had they received his message? What were they thinking of him? Was
Mathieu angry because he had broken his
promise? Did Annette miss him a little? He
cried himself to sleep more than once as he

remembered Grandfather sobbing, "Alone! Alone!"

But when he rose the next day, life was stronger than his trouble. In the morning dew scattered on the meadows, in the glory of the rising sun, in the pools of fresh shade around the great trees, he lost himself, he forgot his anxiety, he became part of the landscape, tramping the dusty roads, resting in the deep grass, eating a crust of bread on the bank of a stream, his burning feet dangling in the cool water. It seemed to him that he discovered a new world. He noticed the plants, he watched the insects and the birds. He followed his way on a map which he had bought, and his little country appeared to him huge and wonderful. He remembered the sea and the fringe of yellow downs, the rich plains of Flanders, the soft hills of Brabant and the high plateaux of the Ardennes. All this was Belgium. All these people working on the land, dwelling in cities, poor and rich, peasants and workmen, Walloon and Flemish, all these people were Belgians like himself. They all belonged to the same huge family. He was

not lost, though an orphan. He was not home-
less, though he had left the wide roof of "The
Three Firs" forever. He had stepped from
one small home into a larger one. He had
only left his house in order to find his country.

He had reached Wavre, a few miles south
of Brussels and was sitting on a bench before
the inn drinking a glass of milk. Through
the windows, he heard the animated conversation of a few men gathered in the bar:

"I tell you the danger is there! It is on the
top of us."

"Pshaw! you've always been a pessimist."

"They would never dare. . . ."

"I don't like the looks of things."

"That's what you always say. You said
that three years ago about the Agadir[14] business, you said it about Algeciras too. . . . And
even if it were war at last! We are not in
danger here. We are neutrals, we have nothing to do with it."

"That remains to be seen. . . ."

"You do not mean to say that they would
invade us!"

"Why not? if it suits their purpose."

The man they called "the pessimist" was interrupted by roars of laughter, but he went on steadily. Pieter listened to him, only to him, with bated breath.

"Why should we mobilize, if there is no danger?"

"To guard the frontier, as in 1870."

"Just a pretext to give them some manœuvres."

"Yes, they like to play soldiers, in the dear old country. . . ."

"I only wish you were right. . . ."

"But we are. What do you think the Germans are made of? Aren't they honest as we are, don't they pay their debts? Don't they honour their signature? We are not the only clean people in Europe. It's all your pride, that's what it is."

Presently the man who had raised this storm came out of the "cabaret." He had a kind, sad face and was folding a newspaper which he thrust into his pocket; Pieter ran after him.

"Excuse me, sir," he said, "but I could not help hearing what you said. I have not read a newspaper for weeks. Could you let me have a look at yours?"

"Certainly, and you can keep it. Only, read it with your eyes open. There are certain things which cannot remain hidden. They must be faced. I fear time is up for many of us."

Pieter did not answer. He was staring at the terrible news. Short of a miracle, war could not be avoided between Germany and France; the decree of mobilization had been signed by King Albert. Belgium was threatened, then. The paper was very comforting, but somehow Pieter could not be comforted. He felt that the old man was right. So, he had scarcely guessed that there was such a thing as patriotism, he had scarcely hoped that the love of country could fill his soul and give him something to live for; and the storm gathered already on the horizon.

Proceeding towards Brussels, he noticed an unusual animation on the road. Soldiers left their houses, with their bundle on their shoulders, women and children stopped on the threshold to wish them good-bye, while requisitioned horses were led out of the stables. But all this was done cheerily; even the women laughed, waving their handkerchiefs in the sun; nobody seemed to think that these preparations might mean anything serious. Pieter met a group of soldiers who were joining their regiment.

"It is a nuisance to be called up just now," one of them said to him, "when there is still so much to do on the land."

"Couldn't they have waited a little longer," laughed another, "until after the harvest?"

"If it were necessary, we should not grumble," added a third one, "but really just to take a walk along the frontier to see that the posts have not been removed. . . ."

The spirit of the Brussels people was just as bright and hopeful. Pieter who had entered the town by the Chausée de Wavre, feeling very tired, stopped in a small "Café" in Ixelles.

"Come to find work?" asked the *baes*[16] who eyed him curiously. "Rather an interesting time, just now. Ever seen the manœuvres before?"

Pieter remarked mildly that he hoped nothing worse would follow. But the man laughed loudly, slapping his thigh. "Nonsense, my young fellow, nonsense! I hope those silly scaremongers have not turned your head the wrong way. Why should anything worse follow?"

"Because the Germans are not to be trusted."

"The Germans!" The big man ran to the bottom of the stairs: "Franz! Franz!"

A voice was heard on the first floor: "Yes, what is it?"

"Do come down."

"I am rather busy."

"Listen, there is a young fellow here who says that the Germans are not to be trusted, that they may invade the country. . . ." There came no answer for some time. "Well," the *baes* roared, "what do you think of that?"

"I think . . . I think that this gentleman must be very young to indulge in such foolish talk."

The accent was unmistakable. Franz belonged to the wronged nation. Pieter blushed and excused himself to the *baes*. He did

not mean to offend anybody. He had spoken
generally.

"That's it, that's it," said the *baes* patting
him on the shoulder, "you spoke without knowing what you were speaking about. But, to-
morrow, when Franz is no longer so busy, you
must have a talk with him. He is a remarkably clever man. He's been my lodger for
four years. Not later than yesterday, he as-
sured me that there was nothing to fear."

"What is his trade?"

"He's a clerk in a large factory. But he
knows many things. He's always calling at
the German Embassy."

And the publican winked at Pieter, meaning
to suggest more than he said.

The next day was a Sunday. As Pieter
came down for breakfast the *baes* was waiting for him at the bottom of the stairs. He
waved a paper in his hand.

"You read that, young man. It will cheer
you up and teach you to abuse the Germans!"

Pieter took the paper and saw reported in
huge print an interview of the German Am-
bassador at Brussels which seemed very reas-

suring indeed. "The house of your neighbour may be burnt down," the Minister had declared, "but your home will be spared."

Surely the man could not have spoken thus, on the eve of hostilities, if he had not known that Belgium's neutrality would be respected. Pieter allowed himself to laugh with the jovial publican at his gloomy presentiments. It was a glorious summer Sunday and, as it was useless to search for work on that day, Pieter decided to see the town. The *baes,* who had developed a sudden sympathy for our hero since he had seen him smile, took him in charge for the day. They went first to the park and Pieter saw at one end of the long avenue of elms the front of the Royal Palace and, right opposite, the House of Parliament.

"They seem to get along all right, don't they?" remarked the *baes.* "There is no trouble for us as long as they live!"

"You mean the King and Queen?"

"We call them Albert and Elisabeth, in Brussels, young man. It is perhaps a trifle familiar, but they would not mind if they knew, I'm sure. How can I help calling him

Albert? Did I not see him running along the Avenue Louise with his brother Beaudouin when they were little boys? I remember, one day, they were laying huge water pipes along the road and, whilst Beaudouin tried to divert the tutor's attention, Albert hid in one of them. I still see the anxious look of the tutor when he noticed that his pupil had disappeared. . . ."

"And Elisabeth—the Queen I mean—what is she like?"

"Come, you are pulling my leg! You are green enough, I see that, but you don't mean to tell me that you know nothing about the Queen?"

"Well, I know that she was a Bavarian princess and that her father was a great oculist, and I have seen some of her pictures."

"Well, you are a provincial, my young friend. Still, rather admit that you know nothing, than pretend that you know the wrong thing—as you did yesterday about dear old Franz's Vaterland. Well, I know many yarns about the Queen, but I will tell you something I saw with my own eyes, two years ago. It happened there, before the palace door. It was a very hot day; the sentry, a grenadier wearing his busby, walked up and down the pavement, in the blazing sun. Suddenly, I saw the man reel and lean against the gate. I rushed towards him, but was stopped by an open carriage which was entering the palace. I saw the Queen leap to her feet and stop the coachman. He pulled his horses up just before the sentry who had grown very pale and looked faint. She jumped out of the carriage and told us to carry him inside. We laid him, with his dirty boots on a brocade couch. She had already got hold of a bottle of some sort and was rubbing his temples softly. He opened his eyes and looked startled, but she said, 'Never mind, keep quiet, do not worry, it will be all right in one moment.' Then she turned towards me as if she did not know what to do. I was afraid to see her fiddle at her purse but she didn't; she saw of course that I was a gentleman. So she simply smiled and said, 'Thank you so much for helping me, Monsieur, it was very kind of you.' She always does the right thing! Of course I just

bowed and went. What could one say? Would
you have said something?"

"I don't see what you could have said."

"Adélaïde—that's my wife—Adélaïde said I
ought to have answered, 'At your service, your
Majesty,' or 'Don't mention it,' or 'Welcome,
my Queen,' or something of that sort. But
Adélaïde is never pleased with me. Well, I tell
you, I could not say anything. I just took to
my heels and flew for my life. But I shall
never forget: 'Thank you so much, Monsieur,
for helping me.' Of course I did not help her,
I helped the soldier. But she knew that I
should be proud to say that I had had the
honour of helping the Queen. So she said it.
She meant also that whoever helped one of
her soldiers—or, for the matter of that, one
of her people—was helping the Queen. Well,
well, she is a small woman—not our Flemish
type, you know—but there is a great soul in
this little body."

The heart of the publican was softened and
his eyes were wet. He sniffed shamelessly and,
taking his companion by the arm he took him
down the Rue de la Régence and the Rue

Royale to show him the sights. They climbed
on the top of the "Colonne du Congrès,"
erected as a memorial of Belgian Independence,[16] and they lingered for some time on the
terrace of the huge Palace of Justice whose
white marble columns glittered against the blue
sky. The *baes* pointed out to Pieter, in the
valley below, the Church of La Chapelle, the
Town Hall's spire, Saint Gudule's towers and,
further west, the many villages which had
now become suburbs of the growing city. And
Pieter, with the great town stretching before
him, understood at once why it should be the
centre of Belgium's national life.

He felt it better still while drinking with
his host in a café of the old market place,
after descending one of the steep streets which
connect the old and the new town, the aristo-
cratic and the popular quarters. There was
something in Brussels air which could not be
found either in Bruges or Antwerp, something
alert, refined, intellectual. Even the diversity
of styles from the old renaissance market-
place to the conventional style of the Park
quarter, to the ultra modern architecture—was

not shocking. The town's atmosphere was strong enough to absorb the most heterogeneous buildings. It was the centre of Government, the centre of learning. Bruges might be Belgium's heart, Antwerp might stand as the symbol of Belgium's body, but Brussels was Belgium's brain.

It was a hot day. This glass of sirop drunk on the pavement of the "Grand' Place" was followed by many others. In the August sun, the gilded houses of the place shone like freshly cleaned copper cans. The *baes* talked constantly about beer, food, politics, Adélaïde's temper. . . .

"By the way," interrupted Pieter, "ought we not to go back and fetch her. You promised, you know?"

But the military band had begun to play the first bars of a march, in the stand.

"Why should we go?" said the *baes*. "The music is good, we are in a shaded corner here. Why should we bother? We are all right. She'll be furious. But that can't be helped. We should be late anyway. You know, much as I like the woman on week days, I can't

"Why should we go?" said the Baes. "The music is good."

stand her on Sundays. You can't please her. That comes from her tight shoes."

"What do you mean?"

"You see, my boy, Adélaïde is a bit coquette. She thinks she has little feet like a Parisienne. But she hasn't. Quite the other way. So, on Sundays—only on Sundays, mind you—she puts on tight shoes which simply torture her to tears. And, as she won't admit the cause of her misery, she will find fault with me. Is that clear?"

They listened to the concert, and a very good concert it was, watching the people passing along in their best clothes, the children playing, the dogs yapping and the contented faces of the peaceful Bruxellois.

"Why should I not be happy, when they are all happy? Why shouldn't there be a small place for me among these people?" thought Pieter. And, as they got up, he sighed: "It is good to be here!"

"I should think so," approved the publican.

When, after climbing the Montagne de la Cour, they got back to the little café, they found Adélaïde, just as they had left her, in

her working clothes. She was not in a temper;
she looked pale and worried.

"What's happened," cried the *baes*. "Anything wrong?"

"It is Herr Franz," murmured Adélaïde.

"Well, what about him?"

"He has bolted."

"Bolted! Impossible! Any luggage left?"

"No, he had been packing since yesterday.
That's why he was so busy."

"A three-months' bill!"

"You shouldn't have let it run so long."

"Who would have thought such a thing of
him, of dear old Franz."

They went on talking about it late in the
night. But Pieter felt troubled about the German's disapearance. It seemed to him a bad
omen.

The Grand' Place
at Brussels

X

LA BRABANÇONNE

THE next morning, at breakfast, the *baes* gave some useful particulars to Pieter and even wrote one or two letters of introduction for some of his friends who might be in need of an extra hand, and it was decided that the boy should at once search for work. It would still be time enough afterwards to inquire about Captain Dierx's whereabouts, as it was not likely that he would be in town or even in Belgium. Pieter had forgotten his presentiments and was greatly cheered by the *baes's* encouraging words: "You need not worry, my boy, you will find something. You look like a gentleman, though your clothes are shabby enough, and you have received a proper education. Everybody can see that. I will answer for your character."

As he was making his way towards the centre of the town, Pieter noticed, however, that the people gathered in small groups and spoke to each other in anxious tones. Once even he caught the word "ultimatum," but thinking it referred to some other country on the brink of war, he did not pay much attention. Suddenly, he saw a news-boy running up the street and, as he went, people flocked around him and anxiously snatched the papers from his hands. Those who had got hold of the news read it aloud to the crowd. There it was, on this damp sheet, fresh from the press, the German ultimatum addressed the night before to the Belgian Government, a demand and a threat. Not the words of the old highwayman: "Your money or your life," but the words of the modern highwayman: "Your honour or your life."

There was no hesitation about the reply.
Pieter looked at the jovial citizens whom he
had seen, the previous day, contented and smiling. The brows were frowning, the lips were
set and the fists were clenched.

"So that's their game," grumbled an old man
beside him. "Well, they'll get our answer soon
enough."

The people around him repeated: "Yes, yes,
let them come, if they dare!" And a dumpy
little woman with a double chin added in a
strident voice: "What do they take us for?
Our honour is not for sale!"

Nobody smiled. There was an extraordinary dignity in the woman's utterance. A
hairdresser was there with his comb stuck in
his hair, a butcher, with his stained apron and
a long knife hanging from his belt, a black
chimney sweep and a white baker, a navvy in
wide velvet trousers, and two little urchins,
their noses in the air, sniffing approvingly.
But nothing was incongruous, nothing seemed
ridiculous. At last, the navvy declared scratch-
ing his head meditatively:

"Well, I am dished if I understand a word

of their lingo. But, if they want trouble,
they'll get it all right. . . ."

As Pieter went further down town, the excitement grew. Anxiety lined many faces, but
the indignation was much too strong to allow
a careful review of the situation. The man
who, coming home at night, is assaulted in his
own house by a burglar does not consider
carefully the inconvenience of facing a pistol
with an umbrella. He strikes back as hard
as he can. That was exactly the feeling of the
Brussels people on this fateful Monday morning. They never thought of their own weakness in the face of the first military power
in Europe; they did not even, at the beginning,
rely so much on the Allies' intervention. The
consciousness of the wrong done to them was
so strong, the implicit faith that right was right
was so vivid, that they took up the challenge
without a moment's hesitation. Absurd as it
may seem, the prospect of prompt victory was
not even questioned; it seemed a matter of
course, like the victory of the boy-hero of a
fairy-tale against the bad giant.

The whole town looked enchanted. People

who would never have spoken together under any other circumstances were seen walking arm in arm. Every political or social barrier disappeared. Strangers exchanged greetings and gripped each other's hands, as if Brussels had suddenly become one brotherhood. The excitement grew every hour. The proud reply of the Belgian Government was cheered in every street, in every café, and when the King, mounting his charger, was seen leaving the House of Parliament, followed by the Queen and the Royal children, the enthusiasm was so great that spontaneously the crowd stopped cheering to sing the "Brabançonne":

"Après des siècles d'esclavage. . . ."[17]

> Après des siècles d'esclavage,
> Le Belge sortant du tombeau,
> A reconquis par son courage
> Son nom, ses droits et son drapeau.
> Et ta main souveraine et fière,
> Desormais, peuple indompté, ·
> Grava sur ta vieille bannière:
> Le Roi, la Loi, la Liberté.
>
> Marche de ton pas énergique,
> Marche de progrés en progrés!
> Dieu qui protège la Belgique
> Sourit à tes mâles succés.

Travaillons, notre labeur donne
A nos champs la fécondité,
Et la splendeur des arts couronne
Le Roi, la Loi, la Liberté.

O Belgique, ô mère chèrie,
A toi nos coeurs, à toi nos bras,
A toi notre sang, ô patrie,
Nous le jurons tous, tu vivras!
Tu vivras toujours grande et belle
Et ton invincible unité
Aura pour devise immortelle:
Le Roi, La Loi, la Liberté!

The men took off their hats and the women lifted up their children in their arms. Was it only that they should see the King or as a kind of maternal offering to this young, proud and simple man who, at that moment, and forever after, embodied the spirit of the nation?

Pieter was literally swept off his feet, carried away by the patriotic devotion of the surging crowd. He felt that he was living a fateful hour, one of those hours which make life worth living and mankind worth loving. He cheered and sang while tears were running down his cheeks. There was a sacred exultation in his heart. The splendid folly of sacrifice had seized him. "Yes, this is my home," he said to himself. "I am no longer alone. All these people are with me. They have given me all, when I had nothing left. I wish to God that I could repay them."

So when the news spread like wildfire that the Germans had crossed the frontier and some men began to march behind a flag, carrying a poster where the words, "Enlist at once" were roughly sketched with a piece of charcoal, he followed the flag round and round the town, until he was so tired that he nearly collapsed on a bench of the boulevards.

He realized that he had not eaten anything since early morning. Should he go back? But would he perhaps then miss the chance of enlisting? A grey-haired soldier was hurrying by.

"Please, sir," cried Pieter. The man stopped. "Please, sir, could you tell me where I must go to enlist?"

The soldier chuckled: "Enlist would you? We don't need children in the army."

"I am no longer a child. I am nearly sixteen years old."

"Well, in any case, you can't do anything to-day. Nothing is organised. Some offices will be open to-morrow I dare say, if you still wish to risk your skin." And the old soldier went away shrugging his shoulders.

When, on his return to the café, the *baes* and Adélaïde heard that he was determined to enlist they overwhelmed Pieter with congratulations: "That's splendid," roared the publican, "only they won't take you, you are too young."

"Too young." The same answer was given him on the next morning when he succeeded at last in entering the recruiting office. A harassed clerk explained to him hurriedly that he could not register him if he did not bring the written consent of his father, or, as he was an orphan, of the people who had made themselves responsible for him. Pieter explained that his uncle was away and that he could not communicate with Marianne. But the crowd was filling the office and the clerk waved him away crying: "Sorry, I can't help it. You might try the military bureau, if you like."

"Pieter ran to the military bureau:

"Show your papers, please," said the sergeant in charge.

"They would not accept me at the recruiting office on account of the date on my birth certificate."

"Quite right. Have you the consent of one of your parents?"

"I am an orphan."

"Of your guardian, then?"

"I have no guardian here." He was so flustered that he forgot to mention his uncle's name.

"That is an extraordinary case. But I am afraid we have no time to examine it. You see we cannot possibly accept a boy under sixteen without some certificate. . . ."

"Please, sir, is there anything I can? . . ."

"I can't take it upon myself. You had better call again when the chief is here."

"Perhaps it will be too late then . . . you will no longer have need of recruits!" Pieter's voice trembled.

"Are you keen about it?"

"It is the only wish I have. . . ."

"Wait a moment." The sergeant stepped

into the next room. "Sorry to disturb you,
sir," Pieter heard him say, "but there is a
boy here wanting to enlist. He is only fifteen
and can't produce his paper. Orphan, I understand, only relation abroad."

"What name?" The voice sounded quaintly
familiar.

"He calls himself Segers, mon major,
Pieter Segers."

Pieter heard a chair falling, and suddenly
on the threshold appeared Uncle Dierx, just
as the boy had seen him, for the last time, on
the deck of the *Léopold II*. He looked older
and his hair had grown grey on the temples,
but Pieter saw only his eager shining eyes.

"By Jove! It is the boy," and seizing him
by the arm, Major Dierx pushed Pieter into
his office. Then, when they were alone, he
shook him by the shoulders and took a good
look at him. "Not changed much? The
image of his mother, but why are you alone
here . . . in such clothes? Where is Marianne? I came back a week ago . . . wired to
old Mestdagh . . . then . . . to that wretched
farm . . . got no answer . . . waited two days.

Was about to start for St. Hubert, when this thing fell on us. Couldn't move, of course. . . . Up to the eyes in work." He explained that, owing to his constant travelling in Africa the news of his sister's death had only reached him when he landed at Antwerp.

He stared at Pieter again, biting his moustache, and finally kissed him on both cheeks.

"And now, you want to enlist. . . . But I won't let you, my boy. What do you know about war! Only fifteen—and not strong."

"Please uncle, I want to, I must."

"We can't discuss that here. Here is some money. Buy yourself decent clothes and meet me to-night at the Hôtel Cosmopolite. Now, run along and—God bless you!"

Pieter was pushed into the street before he knew where he was. He did not buy himself new clothes—what was the use, since he had made up his mind to don the uniform? But he bought a pair of strong boots—which he knew would be useful—and took leave of the publican and of Adélaïde who could scarcely believe his disconnected story. He had great trouble in making them accept his money without hurting their feelings. It was with the greatest difficulty that he tore himself away to keep his appointment at the Cosmopolite.

There, while sharing the Major's dinner, he could speak at last and unfold the whole story of his life at "The Three Firs." He did not mention Annette, of course, and was careful that no blame should be thrown on Marianne and Mathieu. It was merely a matter of money, he insisted. He went away because he understood that Grandfather could not afford to keep him.

"And to think that I never dreamed of all this," burst out the Major, "but now, you must go to the University and go on with your studies."

"I could not, uncle, really, I could not."

A long discussion ensued. The Major used every argument at his disposal—the boy's physical weakness, the hardships of war, the fact that, not being of age, his duty was not at the front. But Pieter, for once, did not give way.

"If everybody reasoned thus," he said, "nobody would enlist. We have all excellent reasons not to fight. Besides, if mother were still here, I should understand, but I am alone. . . ."

"I suppose I don't count," snapped the Major.

"My dear uncle, are you not going to fight?"

"Certainly, I will."

"Well, then, why should I do for you what you are not going to do for me? Let us share the risks."

Uncle Dierx smiled: "You are just as obstinate as your dear mother," he said. "All right, have your own way," and lifting his glass, he murmured, like a prayer: "Long live Belgium!"

"Amen," answered Pieter.

*Belgians attacking in
a Flemish village*

XI

MATHIEU AGAIN

THREE days later, Pieter was drilling in the courtyard of the barracks of Malines. He had been drafted in a regiment of "Carabiniers" on account of his small size, and enjoyed his period of training thoroughly. Some of his comrades were rather rough and some officers did not seem to appreciate sufficiently the generous motives which had prompted these young men to rush to arms in order to defend their country. But, what did it matter? These things became trivial details beside the issue at stake. The weather was glorious; never had Pieter seen such a splendid summer. And the news was good enough to give heart to the worst grumbler of the regiment.

"Oh, to be at Liége," thought Pieter, "to be one of these 40,000 men who hold von Emmich's mighty armies in check!" How many times did they not ask to be sent there, into the thick of the fighting?

But the Commandant only smiled: "Never fear, boys, you will have your turn. In the meantime go on with your drill. I promise to send you as soon as you are ready." And back they went to the parade ground, marching and forming fours as if the fate of Belgium depended on their smartness.

Even when, on the tenth of August, the papers announced that the Germans had entered Liége, the volunteers kept their spirits up. That was only a trick of old Léman to bring the enemy under the fire of his guns. Besides, the papers were not allowed to speak out. Everybody knew, in Malines, that the English had landed in Ostend and Zeebrugge

and that the French outposts had already
reached Brussels. The various successes won
on the Gette, particularly at Haelen, were
greeted with such enthusiasm that the fall of
Loncin had no other effect than to increase
still more the worship which every Belgian felt
for Général Léman. The great battle was at
hand. Belgians, English and French had
joined hands before Brussels, on a front ex-
tending from Antwerp to Namur.. The day
would soon come when the enemy should be
pushed back across the Meuse. And, again,
the men rushed round their officers begging
them to let them go and fight before it was
too late and the war was won without them.
They were so insistent that the old Commandant, biting his moustache, exclaimed:
"Don't be silly, my boys, don't you believe in
these fairy tales. Your turn will come, I tell
you. Every one of us will be wanted." They
went away and some laughed at the "old
grumbler," as they called him. But, on the
next day, the volunteers were ordered to leave
for Ghent. This was the first disillusion.
They spent only a few days there and were

conveyed to Bruges. What did it mean? The
Germans had entered Brussels and Namur had
fallen. Was the country really to be invaded?
But somebody found an article in a Belgian
paper explaining that the line chosen by the
Allies was not on the Dyle but on the Sambre,
so that it was no use defending Brussels any
longer. As for the retreat of the Belgian
army on Antwerp, this was merely a strategic
move in order to divide the attention of the
foe and to oblige him to delay his advance.
Every retreat was "strategic" at that time.

From Bruges, the volunteers reached Brasschaet on foot. They were now behind the line
of the Antwerp forts and nothing, they
thought, could bring about the fall of the im-
pregnable fortress. The training of the recruits, which had been interrupted for a time,
was taken up again. From time to time, they
heard the booming of the guns. During the
first days, Pieter, whose confidence had been
somewhat shaken by recent events, listened to
them anxiously. He was soon able to distinguish between the voice of the Belgian
forts and that of the German batteries. When

the first grew louder, he was filled with joy,
when its booming was intermittent, he was
filled with dismay. Europe's greatest drama
was at that moment played on the Marne, but
the volunteers of Brasschaet paid but scant
attention to that momentous victory. They
had ceased to believe in the papers. All that
was too far away, beyond their reach. They
were much more interested in the sorties of
the Antwerp army and a small advance towards Malines or Termonde took on the proportions of a great success. They clung to
Antwerp as desperate men can cling to a last
hope, without allowing themselves to think
that the town could ever share the fate of
Liége and Namur—that the Belgian army
could be once more outnumbered and out-
gunned. Hope dies hard in the hearts of
youngsters.

One day, the Commandant declared, at the
morning parade, that the 2nd regiment of
"carabiniers" having suffered severe losses
lately, he wanted a hundred men to fill up the
gaps.

"That is a nice way to put it," whispered

a man close to Pieter. But Pieter did not listen to him. He did not even think that if raw recruits were already wanted at the front, the situation must have become rather serious. He had heard his name mentioned by his officer; he had been chosen to defend his country. The hours of tedious waiting were over for him!

The same night, they arrived at a small village near Duffel. The noncommissioned officer who had led them knocked at the door of a dilapidated house. It was pitch dark. A man carrying a lantern answered the knock.

"Is the Major there?"

"Yes."

"I am in charge of a hundred volunteers from Brasschaet."

The man disappeared without answering. They lined up in the road and stood at attention. It began to rain. Pieter's heart was beating in his throat.

Somebody whispered: "What are we waiting for?"

Then the door opened again. At once, Pieter recognized the silhouette of the man

standing erect in the square of light. It was
Major Dierx. He spoke to them kindly.

"Volunteers of the 2nd regiment, I congratu-
late you. You will be able to take your share
of the work of your comrades. Everything
will be new to you. Whatever happens, remain calm and fulfill your orders to the end.
I wish I had not been obliged to call on you
so soon. You have offered your services.
The country has taken you at your word. I
feel sure you will not disappoint her."

Pieter shouted: "Long live Belgium," and
all the men took up the cry.

Major Dierx seemed to hesitate. Did he
recognize the voice? He could not possibly
see Pieter who stood at the end of the line.
Still, he stepped into the road, as if he wanted
to inspect the men. Then, with a sweeping
gesture, he cried: "Farewell, boys, and good
luck to you!"

The door was shut. An officer shouted an
order and the men tramped through the fields
in the direction of the Nèthe.

For two days, the Germans had been trying
to cross the river and had been held in check

by the carabiniers and two regiments of the line. Pieter joined a company which stood in a deep road, well protected by its high banks. A few sentries watched the movements of the enemy while most of the men crouched in the mud below. They were eating when the volunteers arrived and Pieter, who felt very hungry, was just taking his ration out of his knapsack when the bombardment began. The volunteers could not realize the danger at once. They could not understand that such bright fireworks could carry death in their ranks. Some laughed as they saw all the men exposed duck their heads or throw themselves on the ground. But they did not laugh long. A shrapnel burst right in the middle of the road, knocking down four men and, at the same moment, Pieter felt himself pushed down by a strong hand. It was the corporal of his section.

"You must be polite with them, you know," grinned the man, "always make a bow when they come so close."

Pieter saw the dead and the wounded around him and, for the first time, he was afraid. Big shells were bursting in the field behind. The lieutenant shouted some orders; they could not hear him in the uproar.

"You have come in the nick of time," said the corporal, "they have got the range to a nicety. If the forts do not answer soon, this spot will become too hot for any man."

Pieter bit his lip; he felt his legs shaking under him. He longed to do something, to jump forwards or backwards, to charge or to fly. He felt he could not stand waiting there any longer. But, when the order to retreat came at last, he would have given anything to be allowed to remain among the dead and the dying.

The retreat began in good order, the men stopping from time to time to answer the fire of the German infantry, who could be seen advancing cautiously in the dawn. But, when they arrived at the village, they could no longer keep their positions; three or four big shells burst right in the middle of the column. When a crowd of men of the line came running up the street, there was a moment of terrible confusion. Pieter saw his uncle and

two other officers rush into the market place
and shout to the men to walk and to keep their
ranks. At first they did not hear. But Uncle
Dierx jumped on a heap of cobblestones on
the edge of a large shell hole and waved his
sword, exposing himself to the fire of the
enemy who had appeared at the end of the
street. He stood there until the soldiers,
recognizing him, slowed their pace and retired
in good order. Then only, Pieter who had
stopped to watch the major, saw him turn to
follow them. He took three steps and fell
forward. The boy rushed to help him, tried
to lift him up. It was too late; there he lay,
a triumphant smile on his pale lips.

Pieter had, by now, lost all notion of fear
and danger. Bullets were whizzing around him
as thick as a swarm of bees, he did not even
notice them. The sight of the dead hero, the
smell of the powder, had transformed him. His
whole being was rigid with anger. Cool and
composed, he took cover behind the heap of
cobblestones and, aiming carefully, began to
shoot at the Germans who appeared at the end

of the village. Thinking that the ground was
free the enemies rushed through the street.
One, two, three men fell in the distance.
Pieter who had only fired a few cartridges at
the camp-range, was astonished at the result
of his shooting. He did not think it was so
easy. But a great anger was still in him:
"They will not have him, as long as I live.
They are going to pay for this, happen what
may!" He did not even notice that the number of Germans increased and that a Belgian
soldier had joined him behind the barricade.
Suddenly he heard: "For goodness sake,
lower your head, Pieter!" It sounded like
Mathieu's voice. Was he dreaming? He went
on shooting . . . shooting. . . . He had scarcely
ten cartridges left in his belt. "We shall have
to run for it, you know," went on the voice.
"They are going to fire at us from that window." This time he looked round and saw
Mathieu, in the blue uniform of a soldier of
the line, aiming carefully at a window where
some Germans had taken position.

Under any other circumstances, Pieter

"He carried you on his back to the end of the village."

would have marvelled at the coincidence which had brought his friend to his side at such a moment. But he had lost all sense of reality. He just turned towards Mathieu, nodded to him and . . . went on firing. From the window the bullets came closer and closer. He heard again Mathieu's voice urging him to go, then he received a great blow on the head and fell in a dark pit. He fell a long way, so long and so dark was the way that he forgot the time. . . .

When he awoke, a few hours later, in a dressing station, Mathieu was lying beside him.

"What happened?" asked Pieter of the "ambulancier" who was watching him.

"Oh, nothing! . . . He carried you on his back to the end of the village under a hail of bullets. Our chaps, who were counter-attacking, came just in time to pick him up and bring him here. A mad affair, you know. I suppose that means the cross for both of you."

"Shut up, you fool," growled Mathieu. "I only wanted to teach him to keep his promise. We are old friends, you know."

"So we are," whispered Pieter who saw the room dancing around him, "but, tell me Mathieu, how is Annette?"

And he fainted again.

A corner of Ken-sington Gardens

XII

IN THE DUTCH GARDEN

THERE is a corner of Kensington Gardens, in London, a pergola running round two small ponds, which is called the Dutch Garden. Why it is called Dutch, I fail to understand, unless it is because it looks remarkably French. In any case, it is not English and there is a distinctly continental touch about the square basins surrounded with flowers and the two symmetrical lawns stretching before a low building arranged as a shelter, no doubt some dependency of the old palace erected by Wren.

Is it for this, or because the benches against the wall are well protected from the east wind, that the Dutch garden was for months the meeting place of the many Belgian wounded who were nursed in London, during the first winter of the war? It is there that we shall find our friends again, sitting in the sun, on a bright morning in April, six months after the fall of Antwerp.

They are wearing the old blue uniform and the straight képi of 1914. Pieter has still his arm in a sling and Mathieu handles the stick on which he has been leaning. They are smoking their pipes dreamily, watching a patch of yellow crocuses which some thrushes and sparrows are tearing to bits.

"I wonder if she will be able to come to-day," says Pieter.

"She promised to do so. Besides, it is not yet time," answers Mathieu.

"I am afraid she overtires herself."

"She is none the worse for it, anyway. I am thinking more of mother. She must feel terribly lonely over there with the old man."

"What a pity you could not take her along, when you left for Brussels in order to enlist."

"She would not leave him and he, of course, would not leave 'The Three Firs.' "

"Let us only hope that the Boches will not worry them."

"The last news was not bad. They have only taken the horses. Grandfather must have had a fit."

"That was three months ago."

"They are not likely to begin looting and burning again just now."

A blackbird whistled close by, and two wood pigeons alighted at their feet. Some daffodils and narcissus blossoms nodded in the soft breeze. Farther away, the great elms in the Broad Walk were covered with the first green mist of spring. Pieter turned restlessly on the bench.

"Is it not getting late? Should we not go and meet her?"

"Don't you begin to fret. Besides, there she is."

A girl was coming towards them, with a swinging step. Pieter watched her eagerly.

She had the same bright smile, the same light in her blue eyes which used to move him so deeply when they wandered together in the Ardennes woods. But it was no longer the little Annette. She was dressed as an assistant in the Red Cross. She looked graver and self-possessed. She also had been transformed by the war. She shook hands, her lips parted, a little out of breath.

"I hope I did not keep you waiting. I have just received a letter from Maman." She handed it to Mathieu; Pieter read leaning over his shoulder:

My dear little girl:

I am so happy to hear, at last, that you are in safety in England. You must have been through the retreat. What a fearful experience for you, my little girl. I have also heard from my two dear boys. How splendid of them! Has Pieter forgiven me? I wish you would explain matters to him. I was wrong of course. I ought to have accepted Doctor Mestdagh's offer. I undertook more than I could manage, but I did not foresee what would happen with Grandfather. Here, everything is as well as possible, considering the hard times, and we are very lucky compared with others. They have now taken most of the cattle away. I am helping Grandfather in the fields. Being so far from town, we see very little of them, thank God. I am afraid this is the last letter I can send you this way, as it is be-

coming dangerous to write. I will try to send you a card
through Holland, from time to time. Good-bye, my dear,
kiss the boys for me. Look after yourself. God bless you
all. Do not forget me. We will meet again, I feel sure
of it.

Your loving,

Maman.

Mathieu's hand trembled as he folded the
letter carefully. He turned towards Pieter.

"I think you ought to keep it."

Pieter took the letter, kissed it and slipped it
in his pocket.

"I wish Maman could see us," whispered
Annette. She moved towards the pergola.
"Shall we walk a little?" Mathieu took her
arm. He was limping slightly. Pieter followed them. Suddenly she stopped, looking at
the daffodils: "I wonder," she said, "if they
are already out over there. You remember the
spot?" She turned towards Pieter and the
light of spring danced in her eyes.

"Yes, I remember."

"They must look just the same, only they
are wild . . . and you are allowed to gather
them. . . . She laughed. She had not
laughed thus for a long time.

"You know, little sister," said Mathieu, "you owe us that kiss from mother."

She grew suddenly very pale. Pieter's heart was beating fast. She turned towards him questioning: "I suppose I must?"

"Well, since it is Marianne's wish. . . ."

The three were alone in the pergola, alone with their hopes and the spring. She blushed under her cap: "It will be a kiss from the dear old country," she said. Then she took Mathieu by the shoulders and kissed him on both cheeks. Pieter shut his eyes, bending before her. He felt two fresh hands on his face and her lips on his brow.

When he looked at her, he saw a tear running on her cheek.

"Yes, it was just like the old country," he whispered.

NOTES

¹ BELFRY: Every American schoolboy or girl knows Long-
fellow's poem of this famous belfry of Bruges.
"Thrice consumed and thrice rebuilded, still it watches
o'er the town."

² GRIFFON: A little rough-haired dog.

³ BLESSED BOX: The Pyx or case in which the blessed Sacra-
ment is reserved is often made of boxwood.

⁴ BOURGEOIS: In European countries this word is used to in-
dicate a citizen of the middle class; neither a peasant,
who tills the soil, nor a noble, who owns the land, but
a member of the great class between, in which are
found the artisans, merchants, bankers and professional
men, such as doctors and schoolteachers. America,
where we have neither native-born peasants nor
hereditary nobles, is a nation of the middle class or
bourgeoisie.

⁵ PATOIS: A provincial or country dialect of a language.

⁶ CERBERUS: The watchdog of Hades. Most mythologists
say that he had three heads and the tail of a serpent.

⁷ MARSEILLAISE: The national anthem of France. It was
composed in 1792 by Rouget de Lisle and was first
sung by the volunteer soldiers of Marseilles as they
entered Paris. It was forbidden at the time of the
Restoration and during the Second Empire, but it became the national hymn once more at the time of the
Franco-Prussian War, in 1870.

⁸ ROMAUNT OF THE ROSE: A French poem written in the
thirteenth century by Guillaume de Lorris and Jeun

de Meun' and first printed about 1475. Chaucer knew this splendid old poem and translated a part of it into English.

⁹ THE PROFESSOR'S POEM: See the rose
　　　　　　　　Upon which the bee tiptoes,
　　　　　　　　Bend her charming brow—

¹⁰ THE BELGIAN CONGO IN AFRICA: "Congo, and the Founding of the State," by the great explorer Henry M. Stanley, will tell you all about this interesting African country, with its primeval forests, its Pygmy people and its long rivers. Under King Leopold II of Belgium, who established a trading monopoly there, the natives were very badly treated, and the other countries of Europe protested more than once against the cruelty of the Belgian King. But under his successor, the beloved Albert, the Congo, before the Great War, had begun to see happier days.

¹¹ BÉGUINAGE: A kind of nunnery or community house for women.

¹² BRABANÇONNE: The Belgian national anthem was written and composed during the revolution of 1830. A Frenchman Jeuneval (or Dechet), wrote the words; and a Belgian, Campenhout, composed the music.

¹³ ANNETTE'S SONG:
　　　　In my father's garden
　　　　There is a bird,
　　　　A bird in the dovecot,
　　　　A bird in the dovecot,
　　　　There is a bird.

　　　　Every day it says
　　　　That it will fly away,
　　　　That it will fly—from the dovecot,
　　　　That it will fly—from the dovecot,
　　　　That it will fly.

The lovely bird flies
Upon an oak in the wood,
Upon an oak—from the dovecot,
Upon an oak—from the dovecot,
Upon an oak in the wood.

[14] AGADIR: The Agadir Incident, as it was called, occurred in August, 1911, and came near plunging Europe into war. In 1906, the great Powers, or governments, of Europe had held a conference at Algeciras, a Spanish town on the Bay of Gibraltar, to discuss the unsettled condition of Morocco, where the Sultan had been deposed and succeeded by his brother. On April 7, the Powers intrusted to France and Spain the task of quieting Morocco and keeping her at peace. But in 1911, the German Kaiser sent the gunboat Panther down to Agadir, a coast town of Morocco, apparently to interfere in Moroccan affairs. France became very angry at this interference, and a war was threatened, which would also have entangled England. But after prolonged "conversations" Germany agreed to forego her claims in respect to Morocco and to accept instead certain portions of the French Congo, which France ceded to her.

[15] BAES: Boss or Master; the Host of the Inn.

[16] BELGIAN INDEPENDENCE: Until the nineteenth century, Belgium had been a part of the older Kingdom of the Netherlands and had belonged now to Spain, now to Austria, now to France. In 1815 the little country was united to Holland, but the two countries could not get on together, and after the Paris revolution of 1830, the Belgians demanded independence and defended themselves against the Dutch until by agreement the hostilities were suspended while a congress of the five great European powers was held in London. There

it was decided that Belgium should have her independence and should be a constitutional monarchy.

[17] TRANSLATION OF THE BRABANÇONNE:

> After centuries of bondage
> The Belgian, surging from the grave,
> Has reconquered, through his courage,
> His name, his rights and his flag.
> And the hand of this proud people,
> Henceforth indomitable,
> Has written on the old banner:
> King, Law and Liberty.
>
> March on, in your steady stride,
> March on, from progress to progress!
> God, Who protects the Belgian country
> Smiles on your success.
> Let us work; our labour increases
> The fruitfulness of our fields,
> And the splendour of our industry crowns
> King, Law and Liberty.
>
> O Belgium, O dear mother,
> To you we devote our hearts, our arms;
> To you we give our blood, O country,
> We swear it, all, you shall live!
> You shall live always great and bright,
> And your unconquerable unity
> Will take as inevitable motto:
> King, Law and Liberty.

CPSIA information can be obtained
at www.ICGtesting.com
Printed in the USA
BVHW091742070119
537207BV00019B/1261/P